U.S. Department of Justice

I0448598

Expert Working Group Report:
International Perspectives on Indigent Defense

September 2011

NCJ 236022

AUTHORS' NOTE

The group of experts that assembled in late January 2011 came well prepared to discuss the international and domestic practice of criminal indigent defense and the research needed to improve it. As the co-organizers and rapporteurs for the group, we would like to thank all of the attendees for taking time out of their busy schedules and arriving ready to engage the issues. Without their willingness to participate in open and frank discussions, this meeting would not have been the success it was. We also hope the convening expanded and strengthened the network of international experts working on criminal legal aid.

We would like to thank our colleagues at the Access to Justice Initiative (ATJ) and the National Institute of Justice (NIJ), specifically, Deborah Leff, Deputy Counselor for Access to Justice, for her guidance and tireless support throughout the planning of this meeting, and Edwin Zedlewski, the recently retired Director of the International Center at NIJ, for his commitment to our efforts and for ensuring that this convening happened.

We also thank Maureen McGough, Lynn Overmann, Melanca Clark, Karen Lash and Daniel Olmos for all of their assistance in planning and preparing for the meeting and for serving as facilitators for the very important breakout group sessions, and Jonathan Luckett and Matthew Baker for their assistance in locating citations for this report.

Please note that this report does not attribute any comments made during the working group to individual participants. While the report is primarily a summary of the proceedings, in some instances we have included participants' statements unedited.

For more information on the Access to Justice Initiative and its work on indigent defense, please visit http://www.justice.gov/atj/. For more information on the National Institute of Justice and its work in the field of wrongful convictions, please visit http://www.nij.gov.

Maha Jweied, Senior Counsel, Access to Justice Initiative

Miranda Jolicoeur, former International Liaison and Research Analyst, National Institute of Justice

INTRODUCTION

The vast majority of criminal defendants in the United States are too poor to afford a lawyer, yet adequate funding and resources for defense counsel remains an elusive goal. The U.S. Department of Justice (the Department) seeks effective, evidence-based solutions to problems in indigent defense so that the nation can deliver on its constitutionally guaranteed promise to provide legal representation to people accused of crime who cannot afford it.

In January 2011, the Department's Access to Justice Initiative (ATJ) and National Institute of Justice's (NIJ) International Center jointly convened an Expert Working Group (EWG) on *International Perspectives on Indigent Defense* to explore domestic and international practices in indigent defense. That the convening started on the same day that the Governor of Massachusetts announced his plans to overhaul the commonwealth's public defender system was only further evidence of the importance of identifying the best approaches to the delivery of defender services.[1]

The 40-person EWG consisted of leading experts drawn from multidisciplinary communities, including domestic and international practitioners, researchers, government officials and advocates from nine countries.[2] The goals of the workshop were to:

- ❖ Help suggest federal priorities on indigent defense;
- ❖ Help identify research in the field of indigent defense;
- ❖ Learn about alternative and best practices in the provision of defender services for the poor from the United States and around the globe;
- ❖ Consider the transferability of successful international practices to the United States; and
- ❖ Forge sustained American and international collaborations in the field of criminal legal aid.

Over a day and a half, participants were led in a facilitated discussion around the following six panels:

- ❖ The state of indigent defense in the United States generally;
- ❖ Costs associated with being indigent in the criminal justice system;
- ❖ Improvements to the provision of defender services for the poor;
- ❖ Improvements to the provision of defender services for juveniles;
- ❖ The intersection of indigent defense and immigration; and
- ❖ Indigent defense in indigenous communities.[3]

---

[1] Andrea Estes, "Call for Public Defender Overhaul," *The Boston Globe*, Jan. 24, 2011.

[2] Participants came from Bulgaria, Canada, China, Finland, Hungary, the Netherlands, Sweden, the United Kingdom, and the United States. The list of participants for this workshop can be found at Appendix C.

[3] The Workshop Agenda can be found at Appendix B.

At the conclusion of the facilitated discussions, participants were divided into five breakout groups to identify specific, actionable recommendations for ATJ and NIJ. These breakout groups aligned with the panel topics of the convening and were organized to consider **costs** of being indigent, **general improvements** to the criminal justice system, improvements for **juveniles**, special considerations for **immigrants** and special considerations for **indigenous communities**. The breakout groups were asked to create recommendations to advance ATJ's and NIJ's efforts to set federal priorities in indigent defense, identify research gaps in the field and identify international practices that should be assessed for transferability to the United States.

This report provides an overview of the EWG's discussions and includes the breakout groups' recommendations following the summary of the corresponding panel presentations.

ATJ and NIJ were pleased they could foster a new level of cooperation between domestic and international researchers and practitioners in the field of criminal legal aid. Although the level of participation in the EWG is a measure of this new cooperation, so too are the many contacts that have continued after the meeting. This report provides the federal government and the indigent defense community with recommendations that can help steer the direction of indigent defense research and potential reform strategies for years to come.

The authors have included an appendix summarizing the international practices identified in the workshop.[4] No effort has been made to assess whether these practices can or should be transferred to the United States. It is the hope of the authors that assessments of the transferability of some of these practices can be produced in the months ahead.

---

[4] *See* Appendix A, International Practices.

TABLE OF CONTENTS

FRAMING THE ISSUE: THE STATE OF INDIGENT DEFENSE IN THE UNITED STATES

The EWG began with a general discussion on the state of indigent defense in the United States. Participants discussed various problems in the delivery of effective defender services for the poor with the following themes dominating the discussion:

- ❖ Underfunding and the overdependence on judges and politicians who control budgets;
- ❖ Costs associated with remedying cases with ineffective assistance of counsel;
- ❖ Lack of federally enforceable standards on the delivery of defender services for the poor;
- ❖ Excessive caseloads, including the impact of defending misdemeanors;
- ❖ The impact of race on outcomes for clients;
- ❖ Lack of access to experts, interpreters and other crucial resources; and
- ❖ Prosecutorial and police misconduct.

The problem of **limited funding** for public defender offices was a significant concern for the EWG. One participant noted that funding given to state and local agencies often lacks transparency, oversight and accountability. She also noted that due to excessive caseloads, public defenders often struggle to meet their clients even once before trial.

Another participant discussed the **costs** associated with ineffective assistance of counsel, including the costs associated with reversing wrongful convictions.[5] These are often greater than the costs associated with providing adequate counsel in the first instance. She cited the case of Roberto Miranda, who was wrongfully convicted of first-degree murder in Nevada and on appeal, secured a reversal of his conviction and a $5-million judgment against the state.[6] The cost of this reversal and judgment was more than what the cost would have been had Mr. Miranda been assigned competent defense counsel from the outset of the case. Moreover, when factoring in the substantial administrative resources that were expended to adjudicate his claim of constitutionally inadequate counsel, the monetary costs exceeded the $5 million judgment.

One expert discussed cost-savings research from Michigan where the appellate defender office was able to document the cases of criminal defendants that were sentenced to more time than was appropriate because of the inability of defense counsel to effectively navigate the complex sentencing scheme.[7] The white paper computed the cost of that additional time served and compared it with what the cost would have been had the defendant received an adequate defense,

---

[5] On wrongful convictions, see Miranda Jolicoeur, "International Perspectives on Wrongful Convictions: Workshop Report," September 2010, U.S. Department of Justice, National Institute of Justice, International Center, *available at* http://www.nij.gov/topics/courts/sentencing/international-perspective-on-wrongful-convictions.pdf.

[6] *See* Carrie Geer Thevenot, "Settlement Ends Ex-Inmate's Saga, County Insurance to Pay Miranda, Who Spent Years on State's Death Row," *Las Vegas Review-Journal*, June 30, 2004.

[7] *See* written testimony of Dawn Van Hoek, Chief Deputy Director, State Appellate Defender Office, Detroit, Michigan, to U.S. House of Representatives Committee on the Judiciary, House Subcommittee on Crime, Terrorism and Homeland Security, Congressman Robert Scott, Chairman, "Penny-Wise and Pound-Foolish: Waste in Michigan Public Defense Spending," Mar. 26, 2009, *available at* http://www.michigancampaignforjustice.org/docs/DVH%20written%20testimony%203-26-09.pdf.

which could have identified and challenged the errors in sentencing. It was suggested that producing similar studies would be effective in supporting costs associated with defender services, especially given the recent publicity surrounding efforts to reduce prison populations.

Participants also stressed the necessity of **establishing enforceable defense standards** on delivery systems for the legal representation of the poor, which was discussed over the course of the entire workshop. The 2003 NIJ-funded National Legal Aid and Defender Association study demonstrated that standards could have a dramatic impact on quality in the system, but that standards, in the infrequent instances in which they are adopted or imposed, are rarely enforced.[8]

A participant also discussed the effectiveness of public defense pilot programs in Washington State that were developed with limited appropriations.[9] The independent evaluations of these programs demonstrate they reduced incarceration rates and increased deferred prosecutions.[10]

The EWG also discussed the potential advantages of creating a federal ombudsman office, which could receive individual complaints of ineffective defense and could have the power to investigate and recommend relief.[11] Participants noted that the American Bar Association (ABA) supports the creation of independent boards, commissions and ombudsman offices.[12] South Africa's Office of the Public Protector was mentioned as a particularly successful model worthy of study. One participant described efforts in Eastern Europe to emulate the South African office noting its effectiveness as an institution created by, accountable to, and ultimately funded by parliament. (*See* Appendix A, International Practices, South African Ombudsman Model).

The EWG also discussed the impact on **caseloads** of the 1972 Supreme Court decision of *Argersinger*, which required public defender offices to represent individuals in cases involving misdemeanors.[13] In 2007, the Department's Bureau of Justice Statistics (BJS) released two studies on state and county-based local defender offices that confirmed that the caseload crisis in indigent defense is worsening and that misdemeanors are a major factor in increasing

---

[8] David Carroll and Scott Wallace, "Implementation and Impact of Indigent Defense Standards," (Dec. 2003), Award No. 1999-IJ-CX-0049, National Institute of Justice, Office of Justice Programs, U.S. Department of Justice, *available at* http://www.ncjrs.gov/pdffiles1/nij/grants/205023.pdf.

[9] Bill Luchansky, Ph.D., *Looking Glass Analytics,* The Public Defense Pilot Projects Washington State Office of Public Defense (June 2010), *available at* http://www.opd.wa.gov/Reports/TrialLevelServices/1006_PilotProject.pdf. The Washington State Office of Public Defense has also run Pilot Projects Providing Parental Representation in Dependency Proceedings. Evaluations of those projects can be found at http://www.opd.wa.gov/Reports/DT-Reports.htm.

[10] *Id.*

[11] An ombudsman is "[a]n official appointed to receive, investigate, and report on private citizens' complaints about the government," Bryan A. Garner, ed., *Black's Law Dictionary,* 9th ed. (2009).

[12] The American Bar Association (ABA) has a longstanding tradition of supporting the creation of ombudsman offices in the federal government, dating back to 1969. The most recent ombudsman-related ABA policy was adopted in August 2001 and states that the ABA "[(1) s]upports the greater use of 'ombuds' to receive, review and resolve complaints involving public or private entities and [(2)] endorses the Standards for the Establishment and Operation of Ombuds Offices." *See* ABA's Section of Administrative Law and Regulatory Practice Policy page, *available at* http://www.americanbar.org/groups/administrative_law/policy.html.

[13] *Argersinger v. Hamlin*, 407 U.S. 25 (1972).

caseloads.[14] The study found that 15 of 19 state public defender systems reported caseloads above national standards. In fact, between 1999 and 2000, public defender caseloads increased by 20%, while staffing increased by only four percent.[15] And 73% of county public defenders exceeded national caseload standards.[16] The studies found that 43% of state caseloads and 56% of county cases were misdemeanors or low-level infractions.[17]

The EWG also discussed the impact of **race** on the United States criminal justice system. One policy expert stressed that the earliest efforts to improve access to counsel were to alleviate the disparities in the criminal justice system between white and African-American defendants.

She noted that communities of color, including the African-American community, often experience the criminal justice system as discriminatory, where at each stage in a criminal proceeding, there are unique experiences faced by individuals of color: racial profiling, prosecutorial discretion being exercised to punish defendants of color more harshly and underrepresentation of minorities on juries. She stressed that these factors significantly contribute to higher rates of arrests and incarceration of African Americans than their representation in the U.S. population.[18] Black men are imprisoned at a rate of 6.5 times the rate of white men.[19] She linked this reality to the fact that many of the African Americans in the criminal justice system are poor and suffer from inadequate defender services. She noted that these individuals often feel alienated from the criminal justice system because it is managed predominantly by white prosecutors, public defenders and judges. This reality creates racially disproportionate collateral consequences in the criminal justice system, such as the increased need for foster care for black families and the denial of the right to vote to formerly incarcerated black men.[20]

Another important issue discussed by the EWG was the impact of the lack of **resources**, such as experts, interpreters and social workers, for poor defendants. The participants discussed how

---

[14] *See* Donald J. Farole, Jr., Ph.D., & Lynn Langton, U.S. Department of Justice, Bureau of Justice Statistics, *Census of Public Defender Offices: County-based and Local Public Defender Offices, 2007,* NCJ 231175 (Sept. 2010); Lynn Langton & Donald Farole, Jr., Ph.D., U.S. Department of Justice, Bureau of Justice Statistics, *Census of Public Defender Offices: State Public Defender Programs, 2007,* NCJ 228229 (Sept. 2010).

[15] Farole & Langton, U.S. Department of Justice, Bureau of Justice Statistics, *Census of Public Defender Offices: County-based and Local Public Defender Offices, 2007,* NCJ 231175 (Sept. 2010) at 1.

[16] Langton & Farole, U.S. Department of Justice, Bureau of Justice Statistics, *Census of Public Defender Offices: State Public Defender Programs, 2007,* NCJ 228229 (Sept. 2010) at 18.

[17] Farole & Langton, U.S. Department of Justice, Bureau of Justice Statistics, *Census of Public Defender Offices: County-based and Local Public Defender Offices, 2007,* NCJ 231175 (Sept. 2010) at 1; Langton & Farole, U.S. Department of Justice, Bureau of Justice Statistics, *Census of Public Defender Offices: State Public Defender Programs, 2007,* NCJ 228229 (Sept. 2010) at 1.

[18] West, Sabol, & Greenman, U.S. Department of Justice, Bureau of Justice Statistics, *Prisoners in 2009,* NCJ 231675 (Dec. 2010); *see also* The Sentencing Project, "Facts About Prisons and Prisoners," June 2011, *available at* http://www.sentencingproject.org/doc/publications/publications/inc_factsAboutPrisons_Jun2011.pdf.

[19] Peter Wagner, "Incarceration Is Not an Equal Opportunity Punishment," Prison Policy Initiative, http://www.prisonpolicy.org/articles/notequal.html (last updated June 28, 2005).

[20] Alice King, Justice Action Center, *Collateral Consequences of Criminal Conviction: Five-State Resource Guide* (2007) at 14-18.

defender offices are often good models and are usually successful at bringing together the needed resources to provide holistic defense to poor clients. One participant described the Criminal Defense Consortium of Cook County, Illinois, which was created 35 years ago as an alternative to the Cook County Public Defender Office. This consortium of six community-based neighborhood offices was funded by the Department in the 1970s and approached defender services from a holistic perspective using attorneys, investigators and social workers to care for all the legal needs of clients.[21]

The impact of **prosecutorial** and **police misconduct** was also considered by the EWG. Participants discussed the case of Chicago Police Department Detective and Commander Jon Burge, who was convicted of torturing over 200 criminal suspects and forcing confessions while serving as a police officer between 1972 and 1991.[22] Participants discussed the effectiveness of the defender community in Chicago in helping to secure justice for these individuals, many of whom were indigent. One participant noted that due in part to the Burge investigation, former Illinois Governor George Ryan instituted a death penalty moratorium in Illinois. Another participant remarked that the Burge case provides an important lesson for public defenders on the use of international law and procedure. When the investigation was delayed, a petition was filed by victims and human rights lawyers to the Inter-American Commission on Human Rights requesting a hearing both on the facts of the case and on the delay, which was instrumental in creating the political pressure necessary to push the investigation into federal court more quickly.[23]

Many participants agreed that the fact that indigent defendants are a politically weak constituency contributed to these problems. Public defenders and their allies need to continue their advocacy on behalf of this population when new approaches in criminal justice are being developed. One participant cautioned that recent trends in criminal justice, such as restorative justice and the creation of special courts, do not always serve the interests of poor defendants and public defenders must monitor these efforts appropriately.

At the conclusion of the panel presentations, participants discussed their goals for the workshop and provided recommendations to improve indigent defense generally. These included:

1. **Increase Federal Funding for Defender Services.** The Department should increase funding for defender services and assess how funding for indigent defense is distributed through the Edward Byrne Memorial Justice Assistance Grant (Byrne JAG) Program.[24]

---

[21] *See* Randolph Stone, "The Role of State Funded Programs in Legal Representation of Indigent Defendants in Criminal Cases," 17 *Am. J. Trial Advocacy* 205, 217-18 (1993) (describing the creation of the Criminal Defense Consortium of Cook County).

[22] *See* Burge Archive on the *Chicago Tribune* website: http://articles.chicagotribune.com/keyword/jon-burge

[23] *See* University of Chicago Human Rights Program, Human Rights at Home: The Chicago Police Torture Archive, Timeline, *available at* http://humanrights.uchicago.edu/chicagotorture/timeline.shtml.

[24] The Byrne JAG Program, administered by the Department's Bureau of Justice Assistance (BJA), is the leading source of federal justice funding to state and local jurisdictions. The Byrne JAG Program provides states, tribes and local governments with critical funding necessary to support a range of program areas including law enforcement, prosecution and court, prevention and education, corrections and community corrections, drug treatment and

2. **Pass the Justice for All Act.** Congress should pass and fully fund the Justice for All Reauthorization Act of 2010,[25] which includes enforcement authority for the Department's Civil Rights Division to address patterns and practice of constitutional failings in indigent defense systems, provides additional training and technical assistance to help states improve their systems and imposes a comprehensive planning requirement for the Byrne JAG Program which will require that defenders are included in the planning process.

3. **Increase Federal Funding for Evidence-Based Research.** The federal government should fund evidence-based research on the delivery of legal services for the poor, including a review of international efforts to look at the impact of different models and levels of representation. Participants noted that evidence-based research is necessary because it is most effective in persuading special interest groups who do not support increased or enhanced defender services.

4. **Require Better Data Collection.** The Department should collect data to better understand how effective representation can lead to safer and healthier communities, a fairer society and cost-savings by preventing unreasonable, ineffective or unnecessary incarceration. Participants suggested that the Department use its grant solicitation process to gather data on state and local indigent defense spending. One participant mentioned the strains felt by public defender offices in collecting data and suggested that the federal government fund software and technology improvements to assist these offices with case management and tracking as a way to address this problem.

5. **File Amicus Curiae Briefs.** The Department should assist state and local defenders through the filing of amicus curiae briefs in support of legal positions taken by defenders and indigent criminal defendants in lawsuits challenging the delivery of legal services in criminal cases.

6. **Fund Studies on Ombudsman Offices.** The Department should fund studies on the success of ombudsman offices that oversee complaints related to public defender issues to assess whether to establish a federal ombudsman office. Participants suggested that the Department fund studies on how these types of offices are created and their effectiveness.

7. **Launch Effective Public Relations Campaign.** The federal government should launch a public relations campaign publicizing the results of indigent defense research to help change public perception on the need for criminal defense. Participants noted that publicizing exonerations has helped increase awareness of the potential for wrongful convictions. Similarly, they noted the importance of educating judges and prosecutors (and defenders) about client-based indigent defense systems and their benefits. Participants stressed the need to assess the points of view of judges and prosecutors to map a strategy to create support for reform and change that is beneficial for indigent defendants.

---

enforcement, planning, evaluation and technology improvement, and crime victim and witness initiatives. For more information on this program, visit: http://www.ojp.usdoj.gov/BJA/grant/jag.html.

[25] Justice for All Reauthorization Act of 2010, S. 3842, 111th Cong. (2010).

8. **Study the Effectiveness of Standards for Criminal Defense.** The Department should study the effects of implementing and enforcing standards on criminal defense, which have been in existence for nearly forty years.[26]

9. **Increase Federal Funding for Research Specifically to Examine Costs.** The Department should fund research to examine the amount states are spending on indigent defense, corrections, law enforcement and prosecution. Potential research questions include: How much is the federal government giving the states through various grants? What are the disparities in funding?

It should be noted that all of these recommendations were repeated in some fashion at different points in the convening.

COSTS ASSOCIATED WITH BEING INDIGENT IN THE CRIMINAL JUSTICE SYSTEM

The next session explored the economic and non-economic costs associated with incarcerating and sentencing low-income individuals convicted of crimes. Participants discussed the high incarceration rate in the United States, how delinquent youth are handled across systems, the impact of race, the impact of profit motive and the consequences of plea bargaining. The EWG focused on how poverty amplifies these issues and the costs associated with sentences such as the death penalty.

Rates of Incarceration

One researcher provided an overview of the incarceration rate in the United States, which is the highest in the world. Since the mid-1970s, the rate of incarcerating individuals in the United States has increased by well over 300 percent, from around 170 per 100,000 population to 750 per 100,000 population.[27] It was also reported that smaller, but similar changes have taken place in Australia, New Zealand and the United Kingdom.

But divergent trends also exist. Canada's prisoner rates have remained more or less constant, while several Western European countries, such as Germany, France, Switzerland and Belgium, have rates below 100 per 100,000 population.[28] And the Nordic countries — Finland, Denmark, Norway and Sweden — have low rates which vary between 60 and 75 per 100,000 population.[29]

---

[26] *See* National Advisory Commission on Criminal Justice Standards and Goals United States, Report of the National Advisory Commission on Criminal Justice Standards and Goals, NCJ 010865 (1973), *abstract available at* http://www.ncjrs.gov/App/Publications/abstract.aspx?ID=10865.

[27] Tapio Lappi-Seppa, "Exploring the Differences in Incarceration Rates" (Jan. 2011) at 1, unpublished manuscript (on file with the National Institute of Legal Policy, Finland).

[28] Tapio Lappi-Seppa, "Trust, Welfare, and Political Culture: Explaining Differences in National Penal Policies," 37 *Crime & Just.* 313, 316 (2008).

[29] *Id.*

The EWG discussed the reasons for the difference in these rates. One expert argued that the difference could not be explained by rates of crime or victimization in the United States, but suggested it could be the result of weak social welfare policies. In countries with lower rates of incarceration, the disparities in wealth tend to be lower and social welfare programs tend to be more widely available. Therefore, political culture, including trust in government, might explain part of this disparity. But the expert stressed that this would not account for the whole of the disparity between the United States and other Western countries. Instead, it was suggested that the punitive nature of the American public, as well as issues related to race, ethnicity and social discrimination might account for these differences.

As to race, the EWG discussed the disparities in the rate of incarceration based on the race of the offender. A researcher suggested that "ethnic fractionation," or the amount of ethnic diversity in a given society, is often cited as an explanation for differences in incarceration rates, but suggested that in his view political reasons often explain these differences.

The EWG discussed the differences in incarcerating juveniles across jurisdictions. One expert noted that in Finland, there are around five children aged 15 – 17 in prison, as compared to approximately 120 children in the 1970s.[30] This is generally attributed to changes in the child welfare system, including increased efforts to restrict custodial sentences for juveniles.

Another researcher noted that data related to juvenile justice systems in European institutions are often incomplete given the variations in methods used to detain children, such as detention centers, prisons, residential settings and children's homes. For example, placing children in detention centers in the Netherlands has significantly decreased during the past three years, but many of these children are now placed in other facilities while continuing to be deprived of their liberty.[31] So, in fact, the number of children in the criminal justice system continues to increase. The EWG agreed that the careful collection of such data is necessary to draw accurate conclusions.

The group discussed whether the fact that the United States uses private prison corporations might contribute to the fact that the United States has the highest rate of incarceration. It was confirmed by one expert that private prisons are not used anywhere else in the world on the same scale as in the United States. For example, there are no private prisons in Scandinavia, as this would be considered unconstitutional. And while the United Kingdom has some prisons managed by private organizations, these schemes operate in a manner to financially reward a reduction in recidivism.[32] Therefore, studying the use of private prisons would be an important contribution to understanding the unique situation in the United States.

---

[30] Interview with Tapio Lappi-Seppa, Director General of the National Research Institute of Legal Policy. Finland, International Juvenile Justice Observatory (July 21, 2010); *see also* Justice Policy Institute, *Finding Direction: Expanding Criminal Justice Options by Considering Policies of Other Nations*, at 46 (Apr. 2011) (indicating that 6 children in Finland were in secure confinement in 2008).

[31] Plan International, The Netherlands, "Kids Behind Bars," at 78 (Stan Meuwese, 2003).

[32] The expert also noted that the United Kingdom's Ministry of Justice has also begun to look into private involvement in noncustodial sentences to reduce prison populations (i.e., sending prisoners to perform community service instead of serving prison time).

The EWG also discussed the effect of plea bargaining on prison populations. One researcher noted that about 10 – 15 years ago in South Africa, many in that criminal justice community argued that plea bargaining was not available. But research revealed that it was in fact available to defendants with means, who were usually white. As a result of that research and the publicity it generated,[33] the South African Law Reform Commission began to provide trainings to attorneys on how to plea bargain effectively. Interestingly, in Finland there is no plea bargaining, but there are sentencing rules to guide the judge, including criteria for mitigating and aggravating factors such as those related to equity or mercy.

Similarly, in the United Kingdom, there is no plea bargaining, but a defendant can ask for an early indication from the judge as to whether the sentence would be custodial or noncustodial. A defendant can also have a "basis of a plea," where the prosecution and defense stipulate to the core agreed facts, but judges do not have to accept this. Defendants can receive discounts in sentences for early pleas and sentences are generally reduced by a third if defendants plead guilty at the first hearing. The government is considering increasing that to half if defendants plead at the earliest stage, i.e., at the police precinct.

Measuring Costs

The EWG also discussed the process of measuring costs associated with indigent defense. One participant cited a number of studies produced by the Open Society Justice Initiative (OSJI), which examined the cost of detentions in Mexico and Argentina.[34] These studies looked at costs to the state, the individual, the family and the community.

OSJI is also studying the defender systems in Sierra Leone, Ukraine and Indonesia and identified socioeconomic arguments that could be ripe for measurement.[35] In Sierra Leone, OSJI is piloting the use of community-based paralegals to provide legal advice at police stations. Community-based paralegals can be trained and employed more cheaply than trained lawyers.[36] They can also create cost-savings to the community by decreasing the length of pre-trial detention of individuals who would not otherwise obtain legal counsel.[37] (*See* Appendix A, International Practices, Community-based Paralegals in Africa.)

---

[33] Catherine T. Clarke, "Message in a Bottle for Unknowing Defenders: Strategic Plea Negotiations Persist in South African Criminal Courts," 32 *Comp. Int'l. L.J. S.Afr.* 141, 142 (1999).

[34] *See, e.g.,* Open Society Justice Initiative, Global Campaign for Pretrial Justice Report, *The Socioeconomic Impact of Pretrial Detention* (Feb. 2011), *available at* http://www.soros.org/initiatives/justice/focus/criminal_justice/articles_publications/publications/socioeconomic-impact-detention-20110201/socioeconomic-impact-pretrial-detention-02012011.pdf.

[35] *See* Open Society Justice Initiative, "Legal Empowerment for the Poor" webpage at http://www.soros.org/initiatives/justice/focus/legal_capacity/projects/lep.

[36] Vivek Maru, Open Society Justice Initiative, "Between Law and Society: Paralegals and the Provision of Primary Justice Services in Sierra Leone," at 28 (Mar. 2010), *available at* http://www.soros.org/initiatives/justice/articles_publications/publications/between-law-and-society-20100310.

[37] *Id.* at 4.

Another participant noted the development of access to justice measurements at institutions like the University of Tilburg in the Netherlands. Such efforts have begun to measure the private costs that people spend on justice, the quality of the procedure and their perceptions of outcomes.[38] The methodology is being tested in a variety of countries and is also being applied to victims of crime. Ultimately, finding how people think about and perceive justice, including its costs, can lead to better assessments of different models.

Participants turned to discussions on the measuring of costs in a statewide public defender office through the development of caseload standards and the impact of austerity measures on criminal legal aid in England and Wales, where the criminal and civil legal aid schemes have historically been considered strong.

Developing Caseload Standards in Maryland

The EWG next discussed the importance of alleviating high caseloads through better management and staffing of public defender offices. One researcher detailed a 2005 attorney and staff workload assessment of the Maryland Office of the Public Defender (OPD) by the National Center for State Courts (NCSC).[39]

OPD was tasked by the Maryland Legislative and Executive branches to develop caseload standards in order to establish its operating budget. To accomplish this task, OPD worked with NCSC to design a study to measure OPD's attorney and staffing assignments to assess its workload to ensure that the state fulfilled "its constitutional obligation to provide effective assistance of counsel."[40] NCSC designed a project that (1) compiled and inventoried the cases opened by OPD, (2) measured the amount of time that attorneys and staff spent on cases, (3) collected data on sufficiency of time to complete cases through surveys of attorneys and staff, (4) conducted site visits of OPD district offices, (5) convened focus groups of circuit court attorneys district court attorneys, juvenile court attorneys and statewide division attorneys and staff and (6) assigned recommended case weights that were ratified by the OPD Advisory Committee.[41] This project helped to establish recommended caseloads for OPD and importantly, the work had the support of the Maryland General Assembly and the Governor who understood that improving resources for defenders would benefit the criminal justice system.[42]

At the end of the assessment, NCSC found that the public defender office needed about 125 additional attorneys and about 69 additional staff members.[43] In 2003, the Maryland General

---

[38] Martin Gramatikov, Maurits Barendrecht, Malini Laxminarayan, Jin Ho Verdonschot, Laura Klaming, & Corry van Zeeland, *A Handbook for Measuring the Costs and Quality of Access to Justice* (2010), Maklu: Apeldoorn, Antwerpen, Portland.

[39] Brian J. Ostrom, Matthew Kleiman, & Christopher Ryan, *Maryland Attorney and Staff Workload Assessment, 2005*, Maryland Office of the Public Defender, National Center for State Courts, (2005), at 7, *available at* http://www.ncsconline.org/WC/Publications/Res_WorkLd_MDAtty&StaffWkLdAs05Pub.pdf.

[40] *See id*. at 7.

[41] *Id*. at 8-9.

[42] *Id*. at 7-8.

[43] *Id*.

Assembly and Governor endorsed a plan to provide additional staff to OPD over three consecutive years to address the excessive caseloads that prompted the study in the first place. Thus, in 2005 and 2006, OPD was already slated to hire an additional 62 attorneys and about 69 additional staff, partially meeting the need identified by the NCSC study.[44] The study helped educate policy makers about the overall need and made a stronger case for increasing OPD staffing levels. But as one researcher noted excessive caseloads still remain a problem for OPD —and as reported in the most recent OPD annual report available online, in FY 2008, OPD was "42% compliant (5 of 12 Districts) with Circuit Court caseload standards; 25% compliant (3 of 12 Districts) with District Court caseload standards; and 42% compliant with Juvenile caseload standards."[45]

The EWG noted that implementing recommendations to improve offices like OPD often depends on funding considerations and collecting this data is an important first step in making the best case. The ABA's Standing Committee on Legal Aid and Indigent Defense (SCLAID) collected and posted data from all 50 states and the District of Columbia.[46] Maintaining this information is important and participants agreed that finding such data was much easier when it was collected from a central state agency as opposed to municipalities and local jurisdictions.

Both the practitioners and researchers of the EWG also agreed that basic terms such as "case" and "caseload" must be defined consistently across systems and amongst the prosecutor and defender communities to create better comparative data and to assess inefficiencies in resources.

The EWG discussed the impact of plea bargaining on lightening caseloads and whether there is a tendency to plea bargain away cases because of difficulty in the case or under-staffing. A need for better case management systems in public defense systems and in the courts was identified, which could collect data to assess reasons for case closures.

Many participants discussed the need to build quality of representation into workload studies, as was done in NCSC's assessment of OPD. One participant suggested that this could be accomplished by using the established standards on the delivery of defender services when assessing the effectiveness and quality of representation.

The Impact of Austerity Measures on the Legal Aid Scheme in England and Wales

The EWG discussed the criminal legal aid scheme in England and Wales and the impact of proposed austerity measures currently under consideration. The American members of the EWG were particularly interested in understanding the criminal legal aid scheme in the United

---

[44] *Id*. at 8.

[45] *See* Maryland Office of the Public Defender, FY 2008 Annual Report, at 18, *available at* http://www.opd.state.md.us/News%20Assets/annual%20report%202008.pdf.

[46] Holly R. Stevens et al., The Spangenberg Project, "State, County and Local Expenditures for Indigent Defense Services: Fiscal Year 2008," at 9-68 (2010).

Kingdom (and expressed similar interest in the United Kingdom's civil legal aid scheme) given the shared common law traditions between the two countries.[47]

As in the United States, criminal defendants in England and Wales have a right to a lawyer, paid for by the state and can choose to retain a private attorney if they can afford one. In England and Wales, the legal profession is divided between solicitors and barristers—and each have a role in the provision of legal aid on both the defender and prosecutor sides. Lawyers who seek to perform publicly funded work as defense counsel or as prosecutors enter into a competitive process for such contracts, which often leads to highly qualified and experienced attorneys being engaged in the process. Moreover, defense attorneys and prosecutors are compensated at roughly the same levels. It should be noted that while this compensation is generally an adequate salary, it is often less than what can be earned in the private sector.

In the context of criminal legal aid, solicitors can represent defendants in the lower courts, while barristers along with solicitors represent defendants in more serious cases in the Crown Court.[48] Interestingly, barristers also serve as prosecutors and the private bar performs the vast majority of this work, with a percentage handled by public prosecutors employed by the Crown Prosecution Service.[49]

When serving as defense counsel, the barrister's paramount duty is to the court and proper administration of justice with a secondary duty to the defendant, although defense counsel is charged with securing an acquittal for her client. When serving as a prosecutor in a criminal trial, the barrister's role is to present the case fairly and impartially, not to secure a conviction.

Since the 1940s the state has funded the most vulnerable in society in cases involving crimes or family disputes.[50] One participant noted that as a policy matter, the government of the United Kingdom has supported the need for proper defense. In fact, as a signatory to the European Convention on Human Rights, the United Kingdom has acknowledged legal aid as a human right.[51]

---

[47] In the United Kingdom, the legal aid schemes for Scotland and Northern Ireland are run independently of the system in England and Wales. For a comparison of the criminal defense systems in England and the United States, *see* Norman Lefstein, "Criminal Defense Representation in England and the United States," International Legal Aid Group Conference Paper (June 2005), *available at* http://www.ilagnet.org/jscripts/tiny_mce/plugins/filemanager/files/Killarney_2005/Additional_Papers/6.1_Norman_Lefstein.pdf.

[48] *Id*. at 3.

[49] *See* Eurojustice Prosecution in the European Union, Country Report for England and Wales, "The Role of the Public Prosecutor in Court" webpage, *available at* http://www.euro-justice.com/member_states/england_wales/country_report/451/.

[50] For a description of the funding scheme for legal aid in England Wales from the 1940s until today, *see* Roger Smith, "Legal Aid in England and Wales: Entering the Endgame," *International Legal Aid Group Newsletter* (May 5, 2011), *available at* http://www.ilagnet.org/newsletterstories.php?id=37.

[51] European Convention on Human Rights, Council of Europe, § I, art. 6, Nov. 4, 1950, E.T.S., at 5, *available at* http://www.conventions.coe.int/Treaty/Commun/QueVoulezVous.asp?NT=005&CM=8&DF=14/06/2011&CL=ENG.

The government's commitment to funding both criminal and civil legal aid is often cited as an exemplar of state funded legal aid schemes. While legal aid in the United Kingdom is not administered centrally across all four of its constituent countries, funding for legal aid in England and Wales is run by the independent Legal Services Commission.[52] In 2010, the budget for civil and criminal legal aid exceeded £2 billion or approximately $3 billion, but by the 2014-15 funding year, as a result of austerity measures put in place by the government across all agencies, the Ministry of Justice's budget (where legal aid resides) will be cut by 23 percent.[53] Thus, legal aid in England and Wales will have to undergo some substantial changes.

Before reforms are implemented, the government is required to perform a mandatory impact assessment, including their impact on ethnic minorities and indigent defendants. The government will also attempt to quantify the economic impact of cutting funds for advocates.[54]

These assessments are considering the following questions:

❖ What are the fundamental concerns that justify state-funded legal representation? For example, violence, loss of liberty, the welfare of children, the loss of a dwelling?
❖ Should means-testing be introduced for criminal legal aid?
❖ How can the Government introduce more efficient and competitive systems for distribution of legal aid?
❖ How can criminal trials be more cost efficient?
❖ Should family disputes (e.g., concerning access to children) be resolved by judges, or could they be better and (more cheaply) resolved through mediation?

The government had also been considering how to reduce the prison population. In December, the Ministry of Justice issued a proposal to reduce its current prison population of 85,000 by 3,000 in four years,[55] which could result in substantial cost-savings. But in June 2011, the Ministry of Justice abandoned this proposal.[56] Predicting this outcome, one participant noted that the pressure on cutting legal aid funding will intensify.

In an effort to reduce civil legal aid costs, the government is preparing to overhaul civil justice to make the pursuit of claims cheaper and is seeking to introduce new forms of private funding like

---

[52] *See* Legal Services Commission, "What is Legal Aid?" page, *available at* http://www.legalservices.gov.uk/public/what_legal_aid.asp (last updated April 1, 2011). Note that the Legal Services Commission also runs the civil legal aid scheme in England and Wales.

[53] *See* Ministry of Justice, "Proposals for the Reform of Legal Aid in England and Wales," Consultation Paper CP12/10 at 31 (Nov. 2010), *available at* http://www.justice.gov.uk/consultations/legal-aid-reform.htm.

[54] *Id.*

[55] *See* Ministry of Justice, "Breaking the Cycle: Effective Punishment, Rehabilitation and Sentencing of Offenders," Cm 7972 (Dec. 2010); *see also* Ministry of Justice, "Breaking the Cycle: Effective Punishment, Rehabilitation and Sentencing of Offenders," Green Paper Evidence Report, (Dec. 2010); both *available at* http://www.justice.gov.uk/consultations/consultation-040311.htm.

[56] Alan Travis, "Kenneth Clarke Down, Prison Population Up," *The Guardian* (June 21, 2011).

U.S.-style contingency fee agreements.[57] In late June, the government unveiled its Legal Aid, Sentencing and Punishment of Offenders Bill, which upon enactment will implement many of these changes.[58]

Broader concerns include whether cuts in legal aid will seriously impair access to justice and whether in practice downgrading legal aid will cause "ripple" effects (and costs) through the administration of justice.

The Death Penalty

The EWG concluded the discussion of costs with an examination of the death penalty in the United States, which is a unique practice among Western and commonwealth countries. One expert noted that while there is a growing cultural distaste for executions, there is a political inability to abolish death sentencing, which has resulted in a capital legal process in the United States that is cumbersome, slow and extremely expensive.

One expert cited the Brian Nichols courthouse shootings as an example of the inefficiencies in capital cases. That one case in Georgia drained both the financial and political resources of a newly launched statewide public defender system that had taken many years of effort to create.[59]

He further noted that in federal death penalty cases that reach trial, median defense costs now approach nearly half a million dollars per defendant, and federal cases where substantially less money is spent on the defense have been shown to have a much higher likelihood of ending in a death sentence.[60] Most state courts (where the vast majority of such cases are prosecuted) compensate defense counsel for death penalty cases at rates lower than the federal courts, and the death-sentencing rates of many of these jurisdictions are much higher.[61]

The EWG also discussed the usefulness of research examining the outcomes of capital cases as compared to the amount of money spent and the independence of the defense. Examining these correlations would help assess whether life or death in the American capital punishment system

---

[57] *See* Ministry of Justice, "Proposals for Reform of Civil Litigation Funding and Costs in England and Wales Implementation of Lord Justice Jackson's Recommendations," Consultation Paper CP 13/10 (Nov. 2010); *see also*, Ministry of Justice, "Reforming Civil Litigation Funding and Costs in England and Wales – Implementation of Lord Justice Jackson's Recommendations – The Government Response," Cm 8041 (Mar. 2011); *both available at* http://www.justice.gov.uk/consultations/jackson-review.htm.

[58] *See* Suzi Ring, "Government Confirms Jackson Civil Litigation Reforms and Legal Aid Cuts," June 21, 2011, *Legalweek.com*.

[59] Rhonda Cook & Steve Visser, "Murderer Nichols' Tab: $3 Million and Growing," *The Atlanta-Journal Constitution*, July 21, 2009.

[60] Jon B. Gould & Lisa Greenman, Report to the Committee on Defender Services, Judicial Conference of the United States, *Update on the Cost and Quality of Defense Representation in Federal Death Penalty Cases* 25, 44 (2010).

[61] The Spangenberg Group, "Rates of Compensation for Court-Appointed Counsel in Capital Cases at Trial: A State-By-State Overview" (June 2007), *available at* http://www.americanbar.org/content/dam/aba/migrated/legalservices/sclaid/defender/downloads/2007FelonyCompRatesUpdate_Capital.authcheckdam.pdf.

turns on the level of these resources and their allocation, and how lawyers are appointed, trained and organized in capital cases. One participant gave as an example the action taken by Virginia, which historically has had the second highest execution rate in the United States behind Texas. About three years ago, the commonwealth added regional defender offices to handle the majority of its capital cases. Interestingly, since that time, Virginia has not sent anyone to death row.[62] These new offices have been economical and carry a degree of independence,[63] which has been recognized as very important both by the ABA's Ten Principles of a Public Defense Delivery System[64] and by the U.S. Supreme Court.[65]

The expert suggested that by abandoning the death penalty as a viable sentence, the cost-savings to the defense system would be tremendous and the savings could be placed back into defender services to improve the quality of defense for all defendants, regardless of potential sentence. He noted a need for further research to test the relationship between a jurisdiction's indigent defense practices and its rates of death sentences and executions. Another participant suggested that research should be conducted to determine whether states which have eliminated the death penalty use the savings from not carrying out the sentence to provide better defender services.

The great expense associated with death penalty cases stems at least in part from the Supreme Court's insistence on especially high levels of accuracy and fairness in the process by which the death penalty is imposed in any given case. While this insistence has flagged at times over the 35 years of the modern use of capital punishment, recent exonerations of death row inmates appear to have renewed judicial and public support for special care in death penalty litigation. The group agreed that absent a comparable focus on the quality of indigent defender services for non-capital cases, providing adequate resources to the relatively few death penalty cases may have the effect of further impoverishing the criminal defense system as a whole. It was suggested that such imbalances should be recognized as a previously unnoticed cost of the death penalty in the United States.

Recommendations

The breakout group on costs provided the following recommendations:

1. **Increase Federal Funding for Defender Services.** The Department should increase funding for defender services and assess how funding for indigent defense is distributed through the Byrne JAG Program.

---

[62] Virginia Capital Litigation Data Excel Spreadsheet, Virginia Capital Case Clearinghouse, http://www.vc3.org/resources/page.asp?pageid=561.

[63] *See generally*, Virginia Indigent Defense Commission, Annual Report 2008 6-14 (2008) (describing the creation, purpose and operation of the Commission).

[64] ABA Standing Committee on Legal Aid and Indigent Defendants, "ABA Ten Principles of a Public Defense Delivery System," Principle 1 (note commentary at p. 2) (Feb. 2002); *see also* ABA Standards for Criminal Justice: Providing Defense Services (3d ed., 1992) at 5-1.3.

[65] *Strickland v. Washington*, 466 U.S. 668, 686 (1984).

2. **Establish a Federal Clearinghouse.** The Department should establish a federal clearinghouse or center to promote quality indigent defense, best practices and promising approaches.

3. **Fund Studies on the Effectiveness of Standards for Criminal Defense.** The Department should fund studies on the cost of implementing national indigent defense standards together with the cost savings that could result from that implementation.

4. **Study Incarceration Rates across States.** Based on the compelling discussion of disparities in incarceration rates across countries, the Department should perform a study comparing the states with the lowest incarceration rates to the states with the highest rates and identify possible reasons for these differences.

5. **Fund Research on the Effect of Timing of Appointment of Counsel.** Given the lack of information about the attendant fiscal implications, the Department should fund research on the economic impact of the timing of when counsel enters a case from the earliest stage of a criminal investigation (i.e., at the police station during interrogation) on the criminal justice system.

6. **Fund Studies on Recidivism.** The Department should fund studies on the types of charges which generate the highest levels of recidivism and whether incarceration or length of incarceration associated with particular charges (such as non-violent drug offenses) actually increases recidivism.

7. **Fund Research on the Opportunities to Retrain Correctional Personnel.** Should efforts to lower rates of incarceration be successful, correctional personnel would suffer a loss in job opportunities. Therefore, the Department should fund research to assess which careers correctional personnel can transition to most easily.

IMPROVEMENTS TO THE PROVISION OF DEFENDER SERVICES FOR THE POOR

In the next session, the EWG considered innovations that have improved the provision of defender services to low-income individuals both domestically and abroad. Discussion focused on the benefits and costs of more fully integrating private attorneys into the defense bar as in the United Kingdom, possible lessons which could be learned from recent developments in Eastern and Central Europe, the American holistic defense model and the variety of approaches for the provision of defender services taken by the international criminal tribunals.

The Role of the Private Bar in the Delivery of Defender Services

One expert encouraged the development of programs in which private lawyers are substantially involved in delivering indigent defense services in the United States, similar to the system in place in the United Kingdom. The ABA has recognized the need for the involvement of the private bar and has taken the position that public defender offices should only be established when a sufficient number of cases justify these programs.[66] He asserted that without involving

---

[66]ABA Standing Committee on Legal Aid and Indigent Defendants, "ABA Ten Principles of a Public Defense Delivery System," Principle 2 (note commentary at p. 2) (Feb. 2002).

the private bar, legal challenges to caseloads will remain a constant. Also, competition introduced through the private bar creates incentives to perform strong representation in order to gain more client referrals, as is the case in England.[67]

In response to this proposal, the EWG discussed the necessity of providing good monitoring, training and certification processes for private bar members. The San Mateo County Bar Association was highlighted as an organization that effectively trains private bar members to represent indigent criminal defendants through its Private Defender Program.[68]

The EWG also discussed the impact of private bar members who become involved in indigent defense. Private bar members can be effective lobbyists to improve access to quality counsel from the earliest instance in a case and can speak against regressive legislation, such as those concerning the death penalty. But it was noted that private bar members are sometimes limited by the interests of their other clients or by their preference to avoid unpopular causes.

Some practitioners noted that private bar members may be willing to provide monetary contributions or pro bono representation, but in general may not be willing to advocate for legislative change. One notable exception is in Massachusetts, where the Committee for Public Counsel Services, a 15-member committee which oversees the provision of defender services for the poor, has successfully included private attorneys who help to advocate for meaningful change.

The federal defender system was also suggested as a model. It typically has better funding and better private panel representation so that when the federal defender appoints or designates a panel lawyer to handle a case, the client receives effective representation. Moreover, the federal defender office can serve as a resource for private panel attorneys assigned to federal cases, which was cited as one of the reasons the Federal Defender Office for the District of Alaska was created.

In the Eastern European context, moving public defenders into a stronger alliance with the private bar has shifted dynamics such that defenders have begun to feel a stronger connection to the profession and thus guided by ethical responsibilities and standards – improving representation.

The EWG noted two issues concerning the use of private bar members as counsel to indigent defendants: (1) ensuring quality control; and (2) appropriately distributing cases between the private bar and public defender community. Therefore, public-private partnerships, where public defender offices work with private attorneys, and the use of pro bono services in this field should be examined anew to assess these concerns.

---

[67] *See* Norman Lefstein, "In Search of Gideon's Promise: Lessons from England and the Need for Federal Help," 55 *Hastings L.J.* 835, 861-920 (Mar. 2004).

[68] *See* San Mateo County Bar Association's Private Defender Program description, *available at* https://www.smcba.org/News/NewsDetail.aspx?NewsId=3

Criminal Legal Aid in Central and Eastern Europe

The EWG discussed efforts in the European Union and Central and Eastern Europe over the past decade to reform the criminal legal aid system. In 2003, the European Commission, in an effort to establish minimum procedural safeguards for defendants in criminal proceedings within the European Union, issued a statement that while all the rights needed to ensure a fair trial are important, some rights are so fundamental that they should be given priority status.[69] The first priority was the right to legal advice and assistance. If accused individuals have no lawyer, they are less likely to be read their rights and therefore to have those rights respected. This right was deemed necessary to the protection of all other rights. But in 2007, the Commission's work in this area was stopped as it was opposed by several member states.[70] Private advocacy groups decided to carry on this work and provided evidence which documented the degree to which defense rights were provided in practice by member states.[71]

These organizations argued that effective criminal defense is an integral aspect of the right to a fair trial and that it requires not only the right to competent legal assistance, but also legislative support, an organizational structure and a robust legal and professional culture. However good the assistance of counsel is, it will not be enough if the other essential elements are missing.

In the 2008 European Court of Human Rights decision of *Salduz v. Turkey*, the court held that Article 6.1 of the European Convention on Human Rights requires a lawyer to be present from the first time a suspect is interrogated by police, unless it is demonstrated that there are compelling reasons to restrict the right.[72] Prior to *Salduz*, most of the countries in Europe had not recognized this right or if they had, it was not put into practice. As a result of this decision, a number of countries have begun to introduce reforms to implement this requirement. For example, France and Scotland have begun the practice of providing legal advice in police stations during and even before a suspect's first interrogation. Currently the European Union is implementing its criminal justice agenda aimed at adoption of legislative measures for strengthening rights of defendants in criminal proceedings, which includes guaranteeing the right of a suspect to speak with a lawyer.[73]

---

[69] European Commission, *Procedural Safeguards for Suspects and Defendants in Criminal Proceedings Throughout the European Union*, Green Paper from the Commission, Brussels, Belgium, 19 February 2003, COM(2003) 75 final, para. 2.5.

[70] Ed Cape, Zaza Namoradze, Roger Smith & Taru Spronken, *Effective Criminal Defence in Europe* (Antwerp: Intersentia, 2010), at 613.

[71] *Id.*

[72] *Salduz v. Turkey*, 49 EHRR 19 (2009), (holding that access to a lawyer should be provided, as a rule, from the first police interview of a suspect, unless it could be demonstrated, in light of the particular circumstances of a given case, that there had been compelling reasons to restrict this right), *available at* http://www.bailii.org/eu/cases/ECHR/2008/1542.html).

[73] *See, e.g.,* European Commission Press Release, "European Commission to Guarantee Suspects' Rights to Speak With a Lawyer, Inform Family of Arrest" (June 8, 2011), *available at* http://europa.eu/rapid/pressReleasesAction.do?reference=IP/11/689&format=HTML&aged=0&language=EN&guiLanguage=en; *see also,* European Commission's Criminal Justice page, "Rights of Suspect and Accused," *available at* http://ec.europa.eu/justice/criminal/criminal-rights/index_en.htm.

A participant noted that the right to an attorney during an investigation has been recognized in the United States for decades and thus can serve as a model for European countries' efforts as they establish this practice.

Holistic Defense

The EWG next considered holistic approaches to defense – that is, the use of community-based offices which employ a diverse group of professionals (e.g., criminal defense lawyers, investigators, social workers and civil legal service providers) to assist clients with legal and in many cases extra-legal needs. Such a model considers the needs of clients beyond the individual criminal case, with an eye towards addressing the problems that may have led to the individual's arrest including drug addiction or mental health issues. Holistic defender offices, with strong ties to the communities in which they are located and serve, are often advocates for systemic reforms in the criminal justice system that can help break the cycle of arrest and incarceration that have particularly burdened low-income and minority communities.

It was noted that the holistic defender offices are often considered to be more expensive than other types of defender offices. However, overhead costs may be lowered by bringing all services under one roof, and there is some evidence to suggest that clients of holistic defender offices have lower incarceration and recidivism rates as compared to those served by traditional offices.[74] Additional research is needed to effectively evaluate the costs and savings of these offices.

Defender Services in the International Criminal System

The EWG also considered the approaches to the provision of defender services in the international criminal system. One participant provided an overview of the development of defender services in the post-Nuremberg era of international criminal law. He provided an overview of all of the more recently created international tribunals and courts and the evolving placement of the defense unit within these bodies.[75]

Starting with the ad hoc United Nations tribunals for the former Yugoslavia and Rwanda, he explained that the defense unit is separate from the other workings of the tribunals.[76] In these two institutions, the tribunals simply maintain a roster of defense attorneys who have met basic criteria, from which an accused can choose, and who will be compensated from the tribunals'

---

[74] See Melanca Clark & Emily Savner, *Community Oriented Defense: Stronger Public Defenders*, Brennan Center for Justice, p. 14 fn. 13 (2010) (listing studies demonstrating reductions in incarceration and recidivism rates), *available at* http://www.brennancenter.org/content/resource/CODreport/.

[75] For information on the International Criminal Defence Attorneys Association, see http://www.aiad-icdaa.org/index.php?section=1.

[76] *See* International Criminal Tribunal for the Former Yugoslavia's Defence page, http://www.icty.org/sections/AbouttheICTY/Defence; *see also* International Criminal Tribunal for Rwanda, Defence Counsel and Detention Management Section page, http://www.unictr.org/tabid/107/default.aspx; *see also* Association of Defence Counsel Practising Before the International Criminal Tribunal for the Former Yugoslavia, http://adc-icty.org/.

operating budgets. The more recent international courts have refined this approach and the International Criminal Court,[77] the Special Court for Sierra Leone[78] and the Extraordinary Chambers in the Courts of Cambodia[79] have all been formed with an independent defense institution located within the court. These offices certify the defense counsel who can appear before these courts and administer payment of counsel and their teams. These offices also provide limited oversight of case management. And courts monitor action plans to ensure that the attorneys' fees being paid by these bodies are reasonable and appropriate.

The most recently created tribunal, the Special Tribunal for Lebanon, has similarly established an independent institution within the court for defender services, but with even more autonomy than the other courts described.[80] The head of this office is organizationally at the level of a court registrar, which is believed to strengthen the office and increase its independence. Again, defense attorneys must be certified to practice in this court and in fact, the certification process is even more rigorous than in the other courts—requiring applicants to pass an hour-long panel interview. While the case work of this court is still at the very earliest stages, it is envisioned that in addition to the defendant's lawyer, the defender services office of the tribunal will submit briefs on behalf of the accused to maximize the rights for the accused. However, it is unclear what will happen if defense counsel and the defender services office disagree on the theory of the case.

Recommendations

The breakout group on general improvements provided the following recommendations:

1. **Decriminalization.** The federal government should focus on decriminalizing certain conduct in order to decrease pressure on the system and the need for massive funding.

2. **Adopt Enforceable Standards for Criminal Defense.** The Department should create federal enforceable standards, based on the standards produced by the National Advisory Commission on Criminal Justice Standards and Goals, the National Legal Aid and Defender Association and the American Bar Association, which would improve the work of public defenders and outcomes for their clients.

3. **Increase Federal Funding for Cost-Savings Research.** The Department should fund research to study the economic impact of legal aid and public defender offices. Such research should examine the role and involvement of defense attorneys at different stages in a case.

4. **Study the Effects of Competition among the Defender Bar.** The Department should fund research to consider the impact of competition among the defender bar. Specifically,

---

[77] *See* International Criminal Court Defence webpage, http://www.icc-cpi.int/Menus/ICC/Structure+of+the+Court/Defence/.

[78] *See* The Special Court for Sierra Leone Registry webpage, http://www.sc-sl.org/ABOUT/CourtOrganization/TheRegistry/tabid/79/Default.aspx.

[79] *See* The Extraordinary Chambers in the Courts of Cambodia Defence Support Section webpage, http://www.eccc.gov.kh/en/dss/defence-support-section-dss/.

[80] *See* Special Tribunal for Lebanon, Defence Office description, http://www.stl-tsl.org/sid/28.

the research should examine involvement of the private bar and paralegals in the provision of services and how competition can be used to improve the system rather than create additional problems.

5. **Fund Research on the Changing Role of Public Defenders.** The Department should fund research to study the changing role of public defenders, including their workloads, responsibilities and expectations.

THE INTERSECTION OF INDIGENT DEFENSE AND IMMIGRATION

The EWG next discussed the collateral consequences of a criminal conviction for immigrants. The participants discussed the recent Supreme Court decision of *Padilla v. Kentucky* and how best to implement it. The group also discussed alternatives developed by the European regional human rights system and one of its member-states, Sweden.

Immigration Assistance for Indigent Defenders: The Requirements of *Padilla*

The EWG discussed the 2010 U.S. Supreme Court case of *Padilla v. Kentucky*,[81] which held that defense attorneys must inform their clients of the immigration consequences of a criminal conviction, if those consequences are clear (and, if not clear, that a conviction may have adverse immigration consequences). However, one participant remarked that a potential problem with *Padilla* is that it may never be implemented or followed if the resources required by the decision are not made available. Moreover, defense attorneys must have an adequate understanding of immigration law to know whether or not the immigration consequences are clear.

One expert suggested that *Padilla* could best be implemented through training, the distribution of written reference materials[82] and through consultations with immigration lawyers. He discussed three models that public defender offices could follow for providing and delivering immigration support:

- The **central model**, where an immigration expert is centrally located in the town, city or state and can provide training and reference materials and offer consultation to several different public defender offices.
- The **in-house model**, where the public defender office has an in-house immigration expert. (The EWG discussed this model in detail and a lengthier discussion follows below.)
- The **contract model**, where the public defender office contracts with a nonprofit immigration office to provide these services within a jurisdiction.

---

[81] *Padilla v. Kentucky*, 130 S. Ct. 1473 (2010).

[82] *See, e.g.,* Immigrant Defense Project, *A Defending Immigrants Partnership Practice Advisory: Duty of Criminal Defense Counsel Representing an Immigrant Defendant after Padilla v. Kentucky* (Apr. 6, 2010), *available at* http://txe.fd.org/PDF%20files/PadillaPracticeAdvisory.pdf.

The EWG remarked that *Padilla* is legally significant because courts in the United States have resisted recognizing the legal significance of collateral consequences in criminal cases.[83] The group discussed the possibility that *Padilla* may open the door to a discussion about other collateral consequences in criminal cases, including those related to voting, access to entitlements, firearm ownership and professional certification. The group agreed that it is important for public defenders to be able to advise their clients of all collateral consequences, but this is often difficult without training. Participants also indicated a belief that advising on collateral consequences, especially in terms of immigration, should be factored into any defender workload analyses.

The EWG agreed that the NIJ-funded ABA National Study on the Collateral Consequences of Criminal Convictions is a good resource on this issue.[84] The project has catalogued an average of 700 statutes per state or territory that impose collateral consequences on people convicted of crimes.[85] In fact, the Attorney General has sent a letter to every state attorney general asking them to review these collateral consequences and decide which ones are truly necessary for public safety.[86]

The EWG agreed that *Padilla's* placement of the burden on defense counsel rather than on judges was the correct approach. Counsel are in the best position to know the citizenship status of defendants, and attorneys should assess the immigration consequences of any strategy in a criminal case from the very start.

Participants also felt that the advice covered by *Padilla* should include plea negotiation and post-plea advice because that would help clients to understand the process. They also felt that it is important to be creative in terms of resources, specifically examining whether there are academic institutions, nonprofits or private immigration attorneys that will work with the public defender office to provide immigration services.

The EWG discussed the unresolved issues from *Padilla*, namely whether it extends to representation of juveniles and whether a defender is obligated to determine citizenship status of his or her clients. It was agreed that these were areas that would likely become clearer as the law continues to develop.

The opportunity for public defenders to exert pressure on judges in this area was discussed. One participant noted that some judges ask the immigration status of defendants on the record. Given the public policy arguments against that practice, she urged public defenders to intervene when

---

[83] Collateral consequences are consequences that are not part of the criminal sentence but arise or are imposed as a result of a conviction.

[84] *See* ABA Criminal Justice Section, Adult Collateral Consequences Project Site, *available at* http://isrweb.isr.temple.edu/projects/accproject/blog.cfm?RecordID=1.

[85] *See* ABA Criminal Justice Section, Adult Collateral Consequences Statute Demonstration Site, *available at* http://isrweb.isr.temple.edu/projects/accproject/. As of August 1, 2011, the project catalogued 38,012 collateral consequences statutes, an average of 700 collateral consequences per state.

[86] *See* Letter from Attorney General Eric Holder to State Attorneys General, April 18, 2011, *available at* http://www.nationalreentryresourcecenter.org/documents/0000/1088/Reentry_Council_AG_Letter.pdf.

judges ask these questions. Additionally, she cautioned that defenders should continue to advise their clients on all matters, including immigration, even when judges attempt to offer such advice. She suggested that when defenders work with prosecutors, they should consider whether there could be a plea which would avoid deportation and still serve the interests of justice.

Participants agreed that there is an economic argument to *Padilla*. If clients get effective representation earlier on in their case, they are less likely to seek postconviction remedies for ineffective assistance of counsel, which can be quite costly. They felt that if researchers could gather the data and evidence which could back these assertions, it could help encourage the deployment of resources that *Padilla* requires.

The group also discussed the need for adequate interpreter services in defender offices, which is often a necessity in cases involving immigrants. Participants noted that many courts incorrectly take the position that these costs should be passed on to the defendant.[87]

In-House Immigration Experts

The EWG discussed the use of in-house immigration experts at length. At the center of this discussion was the concept of community-oriented, holistic defense.

As in the general discussion of community-oriented defense, participants discussed the costs arguments associated with additional resources in a defender office that practices holistic defense—here, an immigration law expert. But again, participants agreed that the overall cost savings outweighed any initial outputs, such as an expert's salary. The costs saved in not having to train all defenders in the complexities of immigration law could offset the salary of an immigration law expert. Moreover, an immigration law expert can assess immigration issues far more efficiently than criminal defense attorneys.

But participants cautioned that such a model may not be appropriate for all settings. For example, it might not be cost-effective to hire a full-time immigration law expert for a small, rural office. Thus, immigration organizations that help to provide this expertise are equally important, and funding should be increased for these entities. Participants also suggested that factors such as the number of immigrant clients whom a defender office serves and the range of services provided could help determine whether an in-house expert is needed.

An alternative that was discussed was the use of immigration law fellows as in-house experts. For example, fellows like those employed by the Bronx Defenders, could help build a network of trained individuals who can work with both the civil legal aid community and the public defender community.

---

[87] *See* Laura Abel, Brennan Center for Justice, *Language Access in State Courts* at 16 (2009) (describing the practice of court systems that charge interpreter costs and the steps the Department of Justice takes to combat these bad practices). For recent Department efforts on this issue, *see* Letter from Assistant Attorney General Thomas E. Perez to Chief Justices and State Court Administrators, providing guidance to state courts on the requirement to provide meaningful access for limited-English-proficient individuals (Aug. 16, 2010), *available at* http://www.lep.gov/final_courts_ltr_081610.pdf.

International Approaches to Immigration and Criminal Law

Participants discussed the expulsion and deportation of convicted criminals from the perspective of the European regional human rights system and under Swedish law. The European Court of Human Rights and Swedish law consider removal a deprivation of liberty, and, thus, balance a number of interests when determining whether to deport an immigrant who has committed a crime. A number of these provisions require the court to consider the length of stay in the country and the person's ties to the country, especially family ties. In Sweden, if a person has been legally in the country for longer than five years the court will not expel him or her, except under exceptional circumstances.[88] (*See* Appendix A, International Practices, Alternative Practices Related to Immigration and Indigent Defense.)

The EWG remarked that these are very different practices than what is in play in the United States. One participant noted that American immigration law does not consider deportation to be "punishment," nor in many cases does it allow for consideration of individualized circumstances, as in the examples from Europe. She pointed to the 1996 Illegal Immigration Reform and Immigrant Responsibility Act as the primary reason for this approach.[89] The law instituted mandatory detention and deportation of immigrants who committed any crime, ranging from a misdemeanor to a felony. The lack of discretion leads to mandatory deportation without consideration of such factors as military service, length of residency in the United States and whether children or other family members are U.S. citizens. This reality makes the *Padilla* decision all the more important—in order to serve their clients, defenders must consider these rigid and severe immigration consequences when developing strategy.

Recommendations

The breakout group on immigration provided the following recommendations:

1. **Fund Public Defender Offices that Provide Immigration Expertise**. The federal government should fund pilot projects of the various immigration defender models (e.g., in-house model, central model and contract model).

2. **Fund Long-Term Studies on the Different Immigration Public Defender Models**. The federal government should fund long-term studies to identify the cost effectiveness of the various public defender models that provide immigration expertise in light of *Padilla* and how they improve the efficiency of the justice system (by, for example, decreasing the resources needed for litigating ineffective assistance of counsel claims).

3. **Expand Legal Orientation Programs**. The federal government should expand legal orientation programs for individuals held in criminal or immigration custody, especially when they are detained in remote facilities. *Know Your Rights* presentations and direct

---

[88] Exceptional circumstances include an offence that entails serious danger to public order and security, including a danger to national security. *See* Swedish Aliens Act of 2005, SFS 2005:716, chapter 8, §11 (Sept. 29, 2005) and Act amending the Aliens Act 2009, SFS 2009:1542, chapter 8 (Dec. 30, 2009). For an English summary of the 2005 Act and 2009 Amendments, visit this Government of Sweden site: http://www.sweden.gov.se/sb/d/5805/a/66122.

[89] *See* Illegal Immigration Reform and Immigrant Responsibility Act of 1996, Pub. L. 104-208, 110 Stat. 3009-546 (codified in scattered sections of 8 U.S.C.).

representation (particularly for youth and the mentally disabled who are unlikely to be able to represent themselves even with such presentations) are extremely important and should be expanded.

4. **Adopt International Human Rights Standards.** The United States should ratify the Convention on the Rights of the Child, the American Convention on Human Rights and submit to the jurisdiction of the Inter-American Court of Human Rights to enable individuals to access international mechanisms for relief of human rights violations.

IMPROVEMENTS IN INDIGENT DEFENSE FOR JUVENILES

The EWG next discussed juvenile indigent defense in the United States and possible improvements to the system. Participants discussed international law and standards on children's rights, specifically the obligations imposed by the Convention on the Rights of the Child. Participants also discussed alternative and innovative practices occurring around the world in places struggling with a lack of resources for juvenile defense.

The State of Juvenile Justice in the United States

The EWG discussed the "kids for cash" scandal, a judicial corruption scandal involving juveniles in Luzerne County, Pennsylvania uncovered by the Juvenile Law Center.[90] In February 2011, former state Judge Mark Ciavarella was convicted of sending hundreds of children to a private detention center in return for payment from that facility. The fact that these juveniles waived their right to counsel allowed Judge Ciavarella's to easily overlook whether a child's plea was knowing and voluntary. This case received widespread, international attention. One participant noted that the reason for the particularly high publicity may have been due to the fact that the majority of the affected children were white.[91]

Whether every child should have an unwaivable right to counsel, as supported by the National Juvenile Defender Center and National Legal Aid and Defender Association principles, was discussed at length.[92] The consensus was that not only should children have such a right (or at least not be permitted to waive their right until they have had a meaningful consultation with a lawyer), they should have lawyers at all stages of delinquency proceedings.

The EWG also discussed whether states should presume that all juveniles are indigent. Pennsylvania is moving towards this presumption with a growing consensus that a child's right to counsel should not depend on his parents' determination of whether they can or should retain an attorney.

---

[90] Juvenile Law Center, "Luzerne County Kids for Cash' Scandal" (2009), *available at* http://www.jlc.org/luzerne/.

[91] *See, e.g.,* Pennsylvania Juvenile Court Judges' Commission, Pennsylvania Juvenile Court Dispositions at 41-46 (2007) (reporting that in 2007 for all delinquency dispositions in Luzerne County, approximately 64% concerned juveniles were white, 19% concerned juveniles were Latino, and 16% concerned juveniles were African American).

[92] National Juvenile Defender Center and National Legal Aid & Defender Association, "Ten Core Principles for Providing Quality Delinquency Representation Through Public Defense Delivery Systems," Principle 1 (July 2008).

Another issue discussed was the reality of children being tried as adults. Article 37 of the Convention on the Rights of the Child (CRC) states that children who are under 18 should not be tried in the adult system.[93] However, in the United States, children are waived into the adult system and represented by defenders who have limited practice in representing children. The EWG expressed concerns that such defenders often do not have a background in adolescent development, have access to juvenile experts, know how to make use of public safety arguments and know how to keep the children in juvenile court. One of the challenges is to get nonjuvenile defenders to care about and understand these issues and not consider juvenile cases as "practice" for their cases involving adults. One participant noted that research that compared the work of defenders representing adults to their efforts representing children would be informative.

Another participant noted that placing juvenile defense services in the adult public defender offices can create conflict issues. For example, at the conclusion of a criminal case, these offices often cannot represent these same clients in related family court proceedings necessary to reunify families because of conflicts' concerns. The EWG noted that specialized juvenile defender units in public defender offices, like the one that exists in the Philadelphia Public Defender's Office, are a good model and not only ensure that the defenders have the expertise needed to represent juveniles, but also eliminates these conflicts' issues by insulating the attorneys who work on juvenile matters from others in the office.

One participant recommended that juvenile advocates should perform outreach to public defender agencies noting that many of these offices do not prioritize juvenile defense or recognize the need for specialized expertise.

Improving Juvenile Defense in the United States

The EWG next considered improvements to juvenile defense. One participant identified that a key component to the difficulties that exist in this field is the pressure for juvenile defenders to behave like counsel in child welfare matters. And while the lawyers and judges are often the same in the delinquency and dependency contexts, the rules, laws, duties, and standards of proof are different.

A positive development for improving juvenile defense has been the launch of the Juvenile Indigent Defense Action Network (JIDAN) in 2008.[94] JIDAN aims to develop and implement new solutions to improve indigent defense for juveniles and is an "issue-focused forum for the development and exchange of ideas and strategies across states, and for sharing practical information and expertise in support of reform."[95] It operates in eight states and works to improve access to counsel and to create juvenile defense resource centers.[96] The network is

---

[93] Convention on the Rights of the Child, G.A. Res 44/25, *opened for signature* Nov. 20, 1989 (entered into force on Sept. 2,1990), *available at* http://www2.ohchr.org/english/law/crc.htm.

[94] For more information on the Juvenile Indigent Defense Action Network, *see* http://www.modelsforchange.net/about/Action-networks/Juvenile-indigent-defense.html.

[95] *Id.*

[96] The states in JIDAN are California, Florida, Illinois, Louisiana, Massachusetts, New Jersey, Pennsylvania and Washington.

looking at issues of getting counsel at detention hearings, promoting legislation that establishes a presumption of indigence, ending routine, indiscriminate shackling of youth, creating developmentally friendly judicial colloquies, working with law schools on postdetention work and creating Web-based case management systems and collateral consequences checklists.

And like other individuals caught in the criminal justice system, juveniles can benefit tremendously from a holistic approach to solve the problems that created their delinquent behavior. In the juvenile setting, the more resources that are available to children at the beginning of their troubles, their chances of obtaining better long-term outcomes increases. Poor children and their families often are unable to advocate for themselves; therefore, juvenile representation should not be limited to delinquency issues. For example, children often need lawyers to obtain lawful entitlements, such as education services, mental health services, immigration-related services and housing.

In fact, many federal resources exist for children. The U.S. Department of Health and Human Services Administration for Children and Families funds programs that provide services for children and for families of children in abuse or neglect proceedings.

In addition, if children who manifest mental illness or substance abuse are identified at an early stage, delinquency issues might be prevented. Thus, it was suggested that community defenders should reach out to schools and provide training to school nurses and teachers to assist them in identifying these problems. Such training could help schools identify children who are at risk before behavioral problems take root and the children enter the criminal justice system. As a more sympathetic population, more help is available for children than for adults. Moreover, improvements for children in the criminal justice system can lead to improvements for the entire system. The EWG noted that this was a phenomenon found in many countries.

International Legal Standards: Legal Assistance for Detained Children

The EWG discussed international human rights standards and the importance of lawyers for juveniles in the international system. In particular, the EWG discussed the international obligation to provide legal and other appropriate assistance to children who are detained by a state under Article 37 of the CRC, which requires state parties to ensure:

> (a) No child shall be subjected to torture or other cruel, inhuman or degrading treatment or punishment. Neither capital punishment nor life imprisonment without possibility of release shall be imposed for offences committed by persons below eighteen years of age;

> (b) No child shall be deprived of his or her liberty unlawfully or arbitrarily. The arrest, detention or imprisonment of a child shall be in conformity with the law and shall be used only as a measure of last resort and for the shortest appropriate period of time;

> (c) Every child deprived of liberty shall be treated with humanity and respect for the inherent dignity of the human person, and in a manner which takes into account the needs of persons of his or her age. In particular, every child deprived of liberty shall be separated from adults unless it is considered in the child's best

interest not to do so and shall have the right to maintain contact with his or her family through correspondence and visits, save in exceptional circumstances;

(d) **Every child deprived of his or her liberty shall have the right to prompt access to legal and other appropriate assistance**, as well as the right to challenge the legality of the deprivation of his or her liberty before a court or other competent, independent and impartial authority, and to a prompt decision on any such action.[97]

The CRC recognizes the importance of lawyers, who can help juveniles challenge the legality of their detention and even identify alternatives to detention. And importantly, while the child is detained, the lawyer can significantly contribute to the overall objective of a juvenile justice intervention: reintegrating the child into society.[98] Indeed, lawyers serve as liaisons between children and their families in furtherance of Article 37(c)'s protection of a child's right to maintain contact with his family while detained, unless it runs counter to the best interests of the child.

Participants also noted that Article 37(d) recognizes a holistic approach in helping detained children by confirming a right to both legal *and* other appropriate assistance. While the standard has not been read to guarantee access to all important services for children, such as education, international experts noted that the standard is in line with the holistic approaches discussed during the course of the workshop.

The EWG also discussed the applicability of Article 37 in immigration cases. The two leading European Court of Human Rights cases concerning the detention of immigrant minors concerned practice in Belgium.[99] While not concerning right to counsel, these cases concerned the use of detention for immigration purposes and the necessity of detaining minors in expulsion cases. These cases confirmed that the article's scope is broad and can serve as an important tool in immigration cases. (Article 5 of the European Convention on Human Rights, which concerns the deprivation of liberty, is another relevant provision in this context.)

One researcher described the ABA's Rule of Law Initiative's (ABA ROLI) assessment methodology, which considers how to assess judges, lawyers and adherence to international conventions based on international standards. ABA ROLI developed a detention procedures assessment methodology, which allows individuals to examine resources on the right to counsel and detention procedures.[100] The assessments analyze the relevant laws and then look at practice

---

[97] *See* Convention on the Rights of the Child, Art. 37 (emphasis added), *available at* http://www2.ohchr.org/english/law/crc.htm#art37.

[98] *Id.*

[99] *See Muskhadzhiyeva et autres c. Belgique,* Requête 41442/07, Council of Europe: European Court of Human Rights, Jan. 19, 2010, *available at* http://www.unhcr.org/refworld/docid/4bd55f202.html; *Mubilanzila Mayeka et Kaniki Mitunga c. Belgique*, 13178/03, Council of Europe: European Court of Human Rights, Oct. 12, 2006, *available at* http://www.unhcr.org/refworld/docid/4533718d4.html.

[100] *See* American Bar Association Rule of Law Initiative, Detention Procedures Assessment Tool, http://apps.americanbar.org/rol/publications/detention_procedure_assessment_tool.shtml.

using interviews and focus groups. It was suggested that this methodology and the reports completed to date could be useful in examining juvenile detention.[101]

The EWG stressed the need for the United States to ratify the CRC and emphasized its wide applicability.[102] One participant noted that the approximately 8,000 children who arrive unaccompanied in the United States and are detained pending an adjudication of their immigration status could benefit from the strong safeguards of Article 37—especially as it relates to the location of the detention facilities. Although the United States has become more responsive to the needs of these vulnerable children, the placement of the majority of these detention facilities within 250 miles of the United States southern border prevents many of these children from obtaining pro bono assistance. With the facilities located outside of most urban settings, there are not enough attorneys who are able to take on these children's cases pro bono.[103] The justification for the placement of these facilities near the border is that it eases the burden of transferring children between the U.S. Customs and Border Protection, which takes federal custody of the children, and the U.S. Department of Health and Human Services, which houses the children. Thus, if the CRC applied to these detained immigrant children, there would be increased pressure to place facilities in areas that could enable these children to access their right to counsel secured by Article 37.

Alternative Models for Juvenile Defense

One expert noted that the United States shares many of the same constraints and shortcomings as other countries in terms of access to justice for children who are in conflict with the law, but can learn much from the international community's efforts and should adopt international standards—like those flowing from the CRC.

He provided three common areas of concern for most countries and international responses that could provide guidance for the United States. The first is the lack of resources for juvenile defense. Generally, all legal aid systems are understaffed and all formal juvenile justice systems do not take sufficient advantage of informal dispute resolution and enforcement mechanisms as a means of addressing such resource shortfalls. Given that these resource constraints are unlikely to change in the near future, he suggested that new approaches that can augment resources to support the delivery of state-of-the-art services should be considered. Defender agencies are an integral part of this effort in many countries, such as in New Zealand and Canada. In other countries such as Malawi, Ghana, Uganda, Liberia and Sierra Leone, nonlawyers such as paralegals and community leaders are trained to deliver services to children in conflict with the law and to reduce recidivism. (*See* Appendix A, International Practices, Community-based Paralegals in Africa.) There may be certain tasks nonlawyers can perform in the United States

---

[101] These reports and assessments are available at http://apps.americanbar.org/rol/publications.shtml.

[102] The United States signed the convention on February 16, 1995, but has not ratified it. The United States remains one of only two countries that have not ratified the convention — the other is Somalia.

[103] *See* Inter-American Commission on Human Rights, "Report on Immigration in the United States: Detention and Due Process," page 131, Section 379 (stating that the rural location of U.S. detention centers creates significant barriers to legal representation); *see also* Wendy Young & Megan McKenna, "The Measure of a Society: The Treatment of Unaccompanied Refugee and Immigrant Children in the United States," 45 *Harvard Civil Rights-Civil Liberties Law Review* 247 (2010).

without compromising the effectiveness of the representation of children in our juvenile courts.[104]

Another participant noted that in countries with very little resources for public defense, law school clinics are an important resource. More than offering a cost-saving alternative, these clinics can act as a service provider to communities with limited infrastructure. Legal clinics in South Africa funded by legal and were highlighted. (*See* Appendix A, International Practices, Law School Clinics in South Africa.) But the EWG agreed that while it is important to think creatively in using alternative services, they should also proceed with caution because many public defender agencies might be tempted to use inexperienced lawyers, students or paralegals to handle juvenile cases.

The second common area shared across jurisdictions that the expert identified is the lack of due process protections and accurate fact-finding in juvenile cases. Because juvenile cases are often viewed as less "serious" than adult cases, and because in most jurisdictions, juvenile adjudications do not result in findings of "guilt," insufficient attention is paid to due process protections and accurate fact-finding.

The third area the expert identified is the over-institutionalization of youth. Formal juvenile justice systems rely too heavily on incarceration of youth, both pre- and post-trial and youth are often kept with adults in police stations, jails and prisons. He noted that other jurisdictions diverted children from juvenile courts to community-based mechanisms as a means of achieving better, more durable results while at the same time reducing pressure on juvenile courts.

In the context of learning from alternative practices in juvenile justice, the EWG also discussed the European Network of Ombudspersons for Children.[105] This network of 29 European countries provides important services for children, engages in lobbying efforts and shares information to encourage full implementation of the CRC's standards. It is an independent body that monitors the legal and systematic developments concerning children and provides independent monitoring at the local level. Like the South African Ombudsman discussed in Appendix A, these children-related offices can publicly scrutinize the government. It was suggested that such models be considered in the United States.

Recommendations

The breakout group on juveniles provided the following recommendations:

1. **Issue Policy and Advisory Opinions**. The Department should issue a range of policy positions or advisory opinions on juvenile justice to guide states to implement needed reforms, such as a general statement on the nature of juvenile defense, the inappropriateness of waiver of counsel by juveniles, the presumption of indigence of juveniles, the obligations of attorneys to their juvenile clients, the obligation to engage in

---

[104] For an interesting review of the use of non-lawyers in the legal aid scheme in England and Wales, *see* Richard Moorehead, Avrom Sherr, & Alan Paterson, "Contesting Professionalism: Legal Aid and Nonlawyers in England and Wales," 37 *Law & Soc'y Rev.* 765 (Dec. 2003).

[105] European Network of Ombudspersons for Children (ENOC), http://www.crin.org/enoc/.

holistic representation, the obligation for adequate resources for defense counsel and the recognition that the rights of adult defendants apply to juveniles.

2. **Direct Grants Towards Innovations in Juvenile Defense**. The Department should direct grants to catalyze innovation in juvenile defense and to force states to more evenly distribute federal funding throughout the criminal justice system. This should include grants to provide technical assistance for juvenile defenders and to increase data collection.

3. **Fund Legal Representation for Unaccompanied Immigrant Children**. The federal government should fund pilot projects to provide direct legal services for unaccompanied immigrant children in removal proceedings.

4. **Fund Research on Holistic Defense and Diversion for Juveniles**. The Department should fund research on the benefits of holistic representation for children, especially where positive youth development is incorporated. The Department should also fund research on the cost effectiveness of diversion and decriminalization in the juvenile context.

5. **Fund Research on Waiver of Counsel by Juveniles**. The Department should fund research on waiver of counsel in juvenile cases. Research questions should include: Where are children waiving counsel and what are the rates of waiver? What are the outcome differences for jurisdictions that allow waiver as compared to those that do not? What are the benefits to public safety in providing juveniles with counsel? What are the cost savings for states when juveniles are represented?

6. **Adopt International Human Rights Standards**. The United States should ratify the United Nations Convention on the Rights of the Child and other international treaties addressing children and human rights, especially where the right to holistic defense is implicitly recognized.

INDIGENT DEFENSE IN INDIGENOUS COMMUNITIES

The EWG discussed the unique circumstances faced by indigenous communities in balancing traditional and Western forms of criminal justice. The group explored the recently enacted Tribal Law and Order Act and its possible effects on indigent defense in tribal communities, and discussed innovative partnerships between law schools and tribes like the Tribal Court Public Defense Clinic at the University of Washington. The EWG also examined restorative justice approaches as an alternative model to the adversarial criminal justice system and examined some of the practices of Canadian Aboriginal communities.

The Impact of the Tribal Law and Order Act on the Provision of Criminal Defense

One expert gave an overview of the recently enacted Tribal Law and Order Act (TLOA) and its effect on tribal justice systems.[106] The TLOA was intended to address a host of problems in the administration of justice in Indian Country, including lack of funding, the inability of tribes to prosecute serious offenses committed by Indians on tribal lands (and tribes' resulting inability to implement crime control at the tribal level), the complex web of overlapping jurisdictions and the perceived lack of accountability for crime in Indian Country at the federal level. The TLOA grew out of a desire of tribal governments to increase their autonomy and handle cases that would likely not be prosecuted federally. It should be noted that the TLOA does not impose more local control and jurisdiction over non-Indians, but it does put more accountability on the federal government to do its job in prosecuting those cases.

Historically, many criminal defense attorneys were opposed to allowing tribes to prosecute criminal cases because many tribes did not have the capacity to provide defender services. Section 202 of the TLOA accounts for this concern by allowing for enhanced sentencing only when tribal governments can provide substantive and procedural safeguards, including lawyers for indigent clients who face incarceration for more than one year.[107] For tribes that want to take advantage of enhanced sentencing, it also requires that they must guarantee that all defendants receive "effective assistance of counsel at least equal to that guaranteed by the United States Constitution,"[108] the judges presiding over these cases have sufficient legal training to preside over criminal matters and be licensed to practice law by a U.S. jurisdiction,[109] the tribes codify and publish their criminal codes, rules of evidence and rules of criminal procedure[110] and the tribal courts maintain a record (possibly an audio recording) of the criminal proceeding.[111]

Restorative Approaches to Improving Indigent Defense in Canadian Aboriginal Communities

The EWG next discussed the Canadian Aboriginal population which faces similar pathologies and challenges as the Native American population in the United States. In Canada, there are less active tribal law structures than in the United States. Criminal matters in Canadian Aboriginal

---

[106]Tribal Law and Order Act of 2010, Pub.L. No. 111-211, 124 Stat. 2258 (codified in scattered sections of 25 U.S.C.).

[107] 25 U.S.C § 1302(c) (2) requires that an Indian tribe "at the expense of the tribal government, provide an indigent defendant the assistance of a defense attorney licensed to practice law by any jurisdiction in the United States that applies appropriate professional licensing standards and effectively ensures the competence and professional responsibility of its licensed attorneys."

[108] *Id*. § 1302(c)(1).

[109] *Id*. § 1302(c)(3).

[110] *Id*. § 1302(c)(4).

[111] *Id*. § 1302(c)(5).

communities are managed by Canadian Courts and virtually all criminal defense for Aboriginal individuals is handled by legal aid.[112]

One expert detailed the Canadian efforts to find new ways to approach justice problems in Aboriginal areas in order to minimize their contact with the Canadian criminal justice system. Canada has implemented a series of alternatives that exist on a continuum from local grassroots efforts to community-implemented restorative justice processes, even when dealing with extremely serious criminal offenses. (*See* Appendix A, International Practices, Restorative Justice for Aboriginal Communities in Canada.)

Court processes for Aboriginal people fall into three categories: (1) Gladue courts,[113] (2) indigenized courts,[114] and (3) itinerant courts.[115] Each has its strengths and each continues to be improved. To be effective, however, each system requires adequate training for court personnel, sufficient funding, oversight and safeguards for victims and their families.

One participant noted that these efforts can empower Aboriginal communities, which are often disenfranchised from the greater, Canadian criminal justice system. In many Aboriginal communities, the system appears too lenient because offenders who are convicted and incarcerated are often handled by a process that is removed from the Aboriginal community. Minimal efforts are made to engage the community in these mainstream processes, so it appears as if offenders have simply disappeared for a few years. When offenders return to the community at the completion of their sentence, it appears as if there was no accountability to the community at large. Thus, restorative justice processes not only provide an opportunity for communities to take responsibility for their own problems, but to allow for a process of healing.

Participants discussed the degree to which the indigenous legal system is driven by traditions and culture. They discussed the difficulties in trying to implement justice programs in cultures where there might be different views of justice. One participant noted that, like the United States, the Canadian government spent the first half of its history with Aboriginal peoples in an attempt to eradicate traditional processes. But as in the United States, Canada has started to change this approach and efforts to engage traditional responses to justice have increased. Given the relative newness of this approach, difficulties still exist and so the Canadian government is also working to refine its common law system to be more user-friendly to its indigenous community by employing more Aboriginal people in its courts.

---

[112] In Canada, defendants apply for legal aid and, if they qualify, they receive a certificate for legal aid and can then find their own lawyer.

[113] In Gladue courts, court-personnel obtain extensive training on Aboriginal communities and the reasons why Aboriginal people are overrepresented in the criminal justice system. The Gladue workers create a comprehensive pre-sentencing report, which includes information obtained through meetings with family members and community members, and work with offenders to resolve their problems to prevent recidivism. For more information on the Gladue Courts, *see* Appendix A, International Practices, Restorative Justice in Canada.

[114] Indigenized courts function like other Canadian courts but are staffed entirely by Aboriginal people.

[115] Itinerant courts are mobile and can go into communities, such as the Aboriginal communities.

Defender Services in U.S. Tribal Courts

The EWG next discussed the successes in providing effective defender services in tribal courts in the United States and focused on the Tribal Court Public Defense Clinic at the University of Washington. The clinic was formed in July 2002 out of an effort of the Tulalip Tribes to find an innovative way to provide public defender services in its court, which it was not obligated to do.[116] Today, the clinic partners with the Tulalip, Squaxin Island, Port Gamble S'Klallam and Puyallup Tribes to serve as the public defender in their courts.

The majority of the work of the clinic is with the Tulalip Tribal Court where the clinic has handled over 800 cases, with the assistance of four attorneys and 4-16 students each semester.[117] The clinic provides direct public defense to four tribal courts and as much indirect support to tribal public defenders as possible.[118] The clinic is a part of the Native American Law Center, which has met with delegations from Afghanistan about defender services within an indigenous context.

Another participant noted that the current state of public defense in Indian Country is based on the history of tribes and criminal justice. Historically, tribes' justice processes were restorative or restitution based. The current tribal court model is based more on a Western, adversarial model and consists of a judge (who may or may not be trained in law) and a prosecutor who is often an attorney, but rarely does it include a public defender. He noted that he is seeing a change among those tribes that are able to generate funds through economic development (because tribes do not have the ability to tax non-Indians and non-Indian businesses), but unfortunately many tribes are still in economically depressed areas. While it is important to require representation where incarceration might be ordered, it could be devastating to underresourced tribes to require public defense without providing funding.

He also suggested that special focus be placed on the availability of treatment for offenders including evidence-based research on treatment. Such research would assist the criminal justice system in Indian Country. He also suggested that the Department provide longer grant periods and fund the creation of centers of excellence.

Related Civil Issues

The EWG also discussed civil legal issues in tribal communities, which is an area where tribes have more control over their communities than in the criminal context.

In Indian Country, a number of tribal courts have strong civil legal systems. One participant expressed the belief that this empowers tribal governments to resolve problems for their community. However, the problem is that as in the criminal context, invoking civil jurisdiction is

---

[116] *See* Wendy Church, "Why Does the Tribe Use the UW Tribal Court Public Defense Clinic?" (2009), *available at* http://www.tulaliptribes-nsn.gov/Portals/0/pdf/departments/tribal_court/Why-Does-the-Tribe-Use-the-UW-Tribal-Court-Public-Defense-Clinic.pdf.

[117] *See* University of Washington, School of Law, Tribal Court Public Defense Clinic website, *available at* http://www.law.washington.edu/Clinics/Tribal/.

[118] *Id.*

complicated. This can be traced to a line of decisions of the U.S. Supreme Court, which have weakened tribal authority. In *Oliphant v. Suquamish Indian Tribe*,[119] the Court held that non-Indians involved in criminal conduct in Indian Country cannot be prosecuted by tribal courts. Thus, tribes are dependent upon federal or state prosecutors to pursue many criminal cases in Indian County, which is an infrequent occurrence.[120] Consequently, Tribal courts have become very creative using quasi-civil procedures in criminal matters. For example, if a non-Indian commits a crime in Indian Country, tribes may pursue civil actions and seek to confiscate property or impose fines. These processes can empower tribal governments and create a sense of satisfaction among tribal leaders that they can administer justice within their communities.

Another participant felt that one area where tribal jurisdiction is particularly strong is in intramural matters, or internal disputes between tribal or family members, because tribal courts often have strong traditional justice options such as peacemaker courts, mediator courts and elder panels. One participant described a similar program in rural Nicaragua where judges work with lay people in isolated communities to resolve civil, legal problems.[121] Laypersons serve as facilitators for the court system by filing documents and managing the front office. He found that these individuals become important agents of justice within their communities. These processes empowered local communities by training local community members in how to resolve disputes with their own resources.

Interestingly, the experience in Canada is different. One expert remarked that Canada's efforts to support Aboriginal courts and traditional justice have focused on criminal disputes because of the perception that civil matters are less important.

Tribal Juvenile Justice

It was remarked that in the area of tribal juvenile justice, many tribal courts are failing. Washington State tribal leaders met in April 2010 to discuss how to improve tribal juvenile justice. Among the various goals set out at the meeting, the tribes identified reforming tribal juvenile delinquency codes (many of which are modeled on an adult code) as a key priority.[122] Towards that end, the University of Washington's Native American Law Center is developing model juvenile delinquency, truancy and at-risk youth codes.[123]

Participants in that Washington State meeting also discussed enhancing the use of community accountability boards that invoke traditional processes to help reform delinquent youth, such as elder panels or tribal councils. These community accountability boards ask the children to

---

[119] *Oliphant v. Suquamish Indian Tribe*, 435 U.S. 191 (1978).

[120] *See, e.g.*, GAO Report, U.S. Department of Justice Declinations of Indian Country Criminal Matters, Dec. 13, 2010, *available at* http://www.gao.gov/new.items/d11167r.pdf.

[121] See Edward Quintanilla, "Support for the Administration of Justice in Nicaragua — The Rural Judicial Facilitators Program," Scaling Up Poverty Reduction: A Global Learning Process and Conference, Shanghai, China, May 25-27, 2004, *available at* http://siteresources.worldbank.org/EXTGOVANTICORR/Resources/3035863-1291223960989/Nicaragua_Rural_Judicial1.pdf

[122] *See* University of Washington School of Law, Native American Law Center, "Washington State Tribal Gathering: Tribal Juvenile Justice Enhancement" (Dec. 31, 2010).

[123] *Id.* at 23.

discuss how their actions affect the community. One extremely successful program requires the children to construct their genealogy so that they can better understand how the community is interrelated. They are also taught the history of the tribe in an effort to instill pride.

Sometimes young offenders are diverted into restorative processes, such as conferencing or healing circles, but given that lawyers are absent in these types of efforts, due process concerns exist.

Tribes are anxious to intervene well before children are absorbed in the criminal justice system and endeavor to work with schools to stage interventions for students who are truant. Unfortunately, given restrictions imposed by federal education and privacy laws on who can obtain information about students, tribal leaders often find it difficult to learn which students are not attending school. Therefore, some tribes are working within their counties to create tribal truancy boards sanctioned by the county court so that they might obtain information on truant children more quickly and intervene.

Recommendations

The breakout group on indigenous communities provided the following recommendations:

1. **Fund Tribal Public Defender Programs**. The federal government should fund public defenders in tribal court so that tribes can take advantage of the enhanced sentencing authority in the Tribal Law and Order Act. At a minimum, the federal government should fund support and technical assistance to existing tribal public defender programs. As a preliminary matter, an assessment of which tribes are providing public defense must be made.

2. **Establish Centers of Support for Tribes at Law Schools**. The federal government should help to increase the number of centers of support established in law schools, which have been successful in providing technical assistance.

3. **Provide Evidence-Based Services**. The federal government should provide funding for evidence-based services in Indian Country. There are many services available in state courts which have been demonstrated to prove effective in the criminal context; however, most of these services, if not all, are not provided in Indian Country.

4. **Fund Research to Assess Successes in Tribal and Federal Partnerships**. The federal government should fund research to assess criminal justice partnerships between the tribal and federal systems, especially in the pretrial and post-adjudication areas. Research should also be funded to assess reentry of Native Americans post-incarceration into tribal communities.

5. **Evaluate the Benefits of Public Defense**. The federal government should evaluate the benefits of public defense to tribal communities. This could prompt tribal councils to evaluate existing public defense models to measure their benefits, cost savings and outcomes.

6. **Extend Grant Periods**. The Department should extend the time period for tribes to submit grant applications to the Department. Given the extra time needed to clear grant applications through internal tribe processes, such as elder and tribe councils, an additional 30 days would ease the burden of submitting timely and complete grant applications from applicants in Indian Country.

7. **Study the Transferability of Gladue Courts**. The Department should study Gladue Courts in Canada to assess whether they might be transferrable to urban American cities, where the United States had relocation programs for Native Americans.

8. **Study the Transferability of Reintegration Programs**. The Department should study the Canadian model of employing local reintegration workers as case workers for individuals reentering the community to evaluate long-term treatment and to assist reintegration into the community.

CONCLUSION: THE WAY FORWARD

The workshop was a success. In addition to providing specific recommendations to ATJ and NIJ on how to focus efforts to improve the availability and quality of indigent defense, the convening facilitated new collaborations between domestic and international experts in criminal legal aid. Many of the domestic participants noted that the international dimension of the convening was a new approach to addressing the long-standing problems in indigent defense in the United States.

While the EWG provided 40 recommendations to ATJ and NIJ, including suggestions for a potential research agenda, four key themes emerged:
1. Increased **funding** for quality defender services is needed;
2. Enforceable federal indigent defense **standards** should be created and implemented;
3. **Evidence-based research** on the delivery of legal services to the poor should be funded; including the evaluation of successful domestic and international practices; and
4. **International human rights standards** should be adopted.

All agreed that while increased funding for defenders is critical, more must be done than simply find new money for an old problem. The EWG stressed that federally enforceable standards for indigent defendants are needed to deliver on the nation's constitutionally guaranteed promise to provide legal representation to people accused of crime regardless of their ability to pay. And evidence-based research that identifies solutions, including evaluations of successful programs from around the country and the world, could guide policymakers on how to meet those standards. Moreover, the EWG made clear that if solutions could be found from other countries' practice or from international human rights standards, there should not be a reluctance to adopt such practices and standards at home.

While funding is a key component of many of these recommendations, the EWG agreed that if implemented, these recommendations would ultimately save money—both by creating greater efficiencies in the system and, more importantly, by creating opportunities for individuals who come into contact with the criminal justice system to turn their lives around.

The EWG acknowledged the many challenges that exist, including the need to convince the public and policymakers of the need for effective criminal defense for the poor during a time of economic uncertainty. But through their thoughtful discussion and collaboration, the participants provided important recommendations for how the federal government can help alleviate many of these challenges and find a way forward to help improve indigent defense.

APPENDIX A: INTERNATIONAL PRACTICES

This appendix provides additional detail on the international practices discussed at the January 24–25, 2011 Expert Working Group on *International Perspectives on Indigent Defense*, jointly convened by the Department of Justice's Access to Justice Initiative and National Institute of Justice's International Center in Washington, DC. This is not an exhaustive list of international practices mentioned during the workshop, but rather includes those practices that were discussed most extensively. No effort has been made to assess whether these practices can or should be transferred to the United States. The authors hope that assessments of the transferability of some of these practices can be produced in the future.

South African Ombudsman Model

In South Africa, the Office of the Public Protector was created to investigate any conduct in state affairs, or in the public administration in any sphere of government, that is alleged or suspected to be improper or to result in any impropriety or prejudice.[124]

This ombudsman office was established by the interim South African Constitution of 1993 and confirmed as a permanent institution by the final Constitution in 1996. Launched in October 1995, the office of the Public Protector affects jurisdiction over all state bodies, as well as institutions and public entities where the state is the majority owner.

During an investigation, the Public Protector has the discretion to:

- Compel an individual to appear before her to give evidence or to produce any document in his possession or under his control that has a bearing on the matter being investigated and may examine such person for that purpose;
- Request any person at any level of government, or performing a public function, or otherwise subject to her jurisdiction, to assist her in the performance of her duties with regard to a specific investigation; and
- Make recommendations and take appropriate remedial action.

The Public Protector is accountable to the South African National Assembly and must report on her activities and the performance of her functions at least once a year. Any report issued by the Public Protector must be open to the public unless exceptional circumstances require that it be kept confidential.

This ombudsman model has been hailed by many jurisdictions and most recently has influenced the development of similar offices in Eastern Europe.[125]

---

[124] *See* Public Protector of South Africa website, *available at* http://www.pprotect.org/. For a description of the constitutional considerations in creating this office, *see* Jeremy Sarkin, "The Drafting of South Africa's Final Constitution From a Human-Rights Perspective," 47 *Am. J. Comp. L.* 67 (1999).

[125] *See* United Nations Development Programme, Human Rights and Justice in Europe & CIS, "Support to Ombudsman Institutions," *available at* http://europeandcis.undp.org/governance/hrj/show/D468315E-F203-1EE9-B48913F1882228DE; *see also* United Nations Development Programme, Human Rights and Justice in Europe &

Community-based Paralegals in Africa

Several countries with limited financial resources and a limited number of trained lawyers have turned to non-lawyers to assist in the provision of criminal legal aid for the poor. Community-based paralegals or "barefoot lawyers" are non-lawyers trained by civil society organizations with local partners in the formal justice system. The role of community-based paralegals varies depending on the needs of a particular country.[126]

Community-based paralegals may represent indigent clients in local courts, in mediation, or in the formal justice system. They may also educate the community about their legal rights, which can increase citizens' ability to demand change from government and cultivate democratic culture. The legal services provided by a community paralegal may be combined with other social services in the community to add legitimacy to the legal representation. In some countries there are specialized paralegals that focus on criminal justice issues and mainly engage with police stations, prisons and courts.

They can also provide individuals living in rural communities without access to a formal legal system or representation, an opportunity to vindicate their rights. Community-based paralegals can provide representation for indigent defendants in local traditional courts and because they are members of the same community, they often have unique access and knowledge about the needs of all stakeholders in the community. First started in Africa, these programs have spread throughout the continent and to Ukraine and Indonesia.

Community-based paralegals are often used in countries with a shortage of trained lawyers. In **Sierra Leone**, there are an estimated 10 judges and 100 lawyers for a population of about 5 million individuals.[127] Timap for Justice, a local non-governmental organization, partnered with the Open Society Justice Initiative to establish thirteen paralegal offices to help meet the legal needs in the country.[128] The paralegal program combines training, education, mediation, negotiation, community organizing and advocacy.[129] The paralegals negotiate divorce settlements, resolve land disputes and can help hold government officials accountable for their actions in the community.[130] Specialized teams of criminal justice paralegals in three offices assist detainees to secure bail at police stations and through magistrates.

CIS, Ombudsman Creation Acts, *available at* http://europeandcis.undp.org/governance/hrj/show/D4DBEA27-F203-1EE9-B982684BD0814688.

[126] Open Society Justice Institute has created a guide to creating a paralegal program: *Community-Based Paralegals: A Practitioners Guide* (2010), *available at* http://www.soros.org/initiatives/justice/focus/legal_capacity/articles_publications/publications/paralegals-manual-20101208.

[127] Timap for Justice, www.timapforjustice.org; *see also* Vivek Maru, "Between Law and Society: Paralegals and the Provision of Primary Justice Services in Sierra Leone," Open Society Justice Initiative (2006).

[128] *Id.*

[129] *Id.*

[130] *Id.*

Additionally, Sierra Leone operates a dual system, recognizing both formal legal and traditional processes. The community-based paralegals are trained in both formal law and community-based dispute resolution.[131] This enables the paralegals to assist clients in the traditional system with the added knowledge of the defendant's rights under the formal legal system and the ability to assess conflict-of-law issues in the dual system.

In **Malawi**, the Paralegal Advisory Service was initially started to reach prison populations without access to lawyers. Paralegal training courses include criminal law and procedure, interviewing skills and information management.[132] The paralegals provide legal advice and "know your rights" trainings for individuals who proceed pro se.[133] The paralegals also work with different criminal justice agencies in an effort to improve coordination and cooperation between them.[134] The program in Malawi has been adapted and applied in **Benin**, **Kenya** and **Uganda**.

The Malawi program has recently expanded its use of paralegals into other parts of the criminal justice system due to their success in the prison context. Paralegal services are now available in thirteen prisons, covering 84% of the prison population, four court rooms and eight police stations.[135]

Alternative Practices Related to Immigration and Criminal Defense

The EWG learned of alternative approaches in immigration policy when immigrants come into contact with the criminal justice system. In particular, the EWG learned about the European regional human rights system and the safeguards provided to immigrants by the European Convention on Human Rights, as developed through decisions of the European Court of Human Rights, and the practice of one of its member-states, Sweden.

The European Human Rights System

The European Convention on Human Rights (European Convention) contains very few explicit references to non-citizens.[136] As the European Court of Human Rights (ECHR) has made clear on many occasions, the European Convention's obligations on the treatment of aliens do not restrict a state's right to regulate immigration.

---

[131] *Id.*

[132] *Access to Justice in Africa and Beyond: Making the Rule of Law a Reality* (2007), Penal Reform International and the Bluhm Legal Clinic of the Northwestern University School of Law, p. 147; full text *available at* http://www.penalreform.org/files/rep-2007-access-africa-and-beyond-en.pdf.

[133] *Id.*

[134] *Id.*

[135] *Id.*

[136] European Convention on Human Rights, Council of Europe, Nov. 4, 1950, E.T.S. at 5, *available at* http://www.conventions.coe.int/Treaty/Commun/QueVoulezVous.asp?NT=005&CM=8&DF=14/06/2011&CL=ENG.

Nonetheless, the ECHR's case law has developed substantive rights pertaining to aliens under the following articles:

- ❖ Article 2 – providing for the right to life;
- ❖ Article 3 – prohibiting torture and inhuman or degrading treatment or punishment; and
- ❖ Article 8 – providing for the right to private and family life.

As a result of the special character of the protections afforded under Article 3, the ECHR has rarely needed to examine a case under Article 2.

The prohibition on torture and inhuman or degrading treatment or punishment found in Article 3 is not confined to the territory of the contracting state. It also applies in cases of deportation, extradition or expulsion "where substantial grounds have been shown for believing that the person concerned, if extradited, faces a real risk of being subjected" to treatment contrary to Article 3 in the receiving country.[137] This is an absolute rule and does not allow for a weighing of the state's interests against those of the individual. Thus, if the ECHR finds that an expulsion order would violate Article 3, there is an implied obligation of the state to not expel the alien. This is true even when an alien is found guilty of a serious offense or when national security considerations like terrorism are involved.[138] Moreover, this prohibition extends to exceptional circumstances such as in cases where the alien might face the United States' "death row phenomenon"[139] or when an alien has been diagnosed with AIDS.[140]

Article 8 of the European Convention protects the rights of everyone to private life and in particular family life. In cases involving Article 8, the issue is whether a fair balance has been struck between the individual's private or family life and the state's interest in preventing

---

[137] *Soering v. the United Kingdom*, 11 EHRR 439, §91 (1989), *available at* http://www.bailii.org/eu/cases/ECHR/1989/14.html.

[138] *See, e.g., Chahal v. the United Kingdom*, 23 EHRR 413, §80 (1997) (holding "The prohibition provided by Article 3 (art. 3) against ill-treatment is equally absolute in expulsion cases. Thus, whenever substantial grounds have been shown for believing that an individual would face a real risk of being subjected to treatment contrary to Article 3 (art. 3) if removed to another State, the responsibility of the Contracting State to safeguard him or her against such treatment is engaged in the event of expulsion […]. In these circumstances, the activities of the individual in question, however undesirable or dangerous, cannot be a material consideration. The protection afforded by Article 3 (art. 3) is thus wider than that provided by Articles 32 and 33 of the United Nations 1951 Convention on the Status of Refugees […],"*available at* http://www.bailii.org/eu/cases/ECHR/1996/54.html.

[139] *Soering v. the United Kingdom*, 11 EHRR 439, §111 (holding "[I]n the Court's view, having regard to the very long period of time spent on death row in such extreme conditions, with the ever present and mounting anguish of awaiting execution of the death penalty, and to the personal circumstances of the applicant, especially his age and mental state at the time of the offence, the applicant's extradition to the United States would expose him to a real risk of treatment going beyond the threshold set by Article 3 (art. 3). A further consideration of relevance is that in the particular instance the legitimate purpose of extradition could be achieved by another means which would not involve suffering of such exceptional intensity or duration. Accordingly, the [United Kingdom's] Secretary of State's decision to extradite the applicant to the United States would, if implemented, give rise to a breach of Article 3 (art. 3)," *available at* http://www.bailii.org/eu/cases/ECHR/1989/14.html.

[140] *D. v. the United Kingdom*, 24 EHRR 423 (1997) (holding that the United Kingdom's deportation order violated Article 3 of the European Convention on Human Rights because the applicant was diagnosed with AIDS and would receive inferior medical treatment in his home country of St. Kitts), *available at* http://www.bailii.org/eu/cases/ECHR/1997/25.html.

disorder or crime. The ECHR has established certain criteria for the balancing of these interests; however, it has not indicated the relative weight to be given to each. It will consider the nature and seriousness of the offense, the length of stay in the expelling country, the time that has passed since the offense was committed, the best interests of children and the strength of social, cultural and family ties both within the host country and the country of destination. The criteria that usually favor individuals the most are family situation and length of stay in the country.

Nevertheless, the ECHR has made clear that there is no absolute right for immigrants "not to be expelled."[141]

Swedish Law and Practice

The Swedish rules governing the expulsion of convicted immigrants are found in the Aliens Act of 2005, as amended in 2009.[142]

The decision whether to issue a removal order of an immigrant convicted of a crime rests with the criminal court. Under Swedish law, such an order is not characterized as a criminal penalty but is a "special legal consequence" of the crime.[143] The court takes into account the consequences of an expulsion and can reduce the penalty accordingly. Generally, an expulsion order is combined with a prohibition of the non-citizen's return to Sweden, either for a limited duration (normally five or ten years) or indefinitely.

The Aliens Act also sets conditions for expulsion of a convicted immigrant.[144] First, the immigrant must have committed a crime of such seriousness that it could lead to imprisonment. Second, either there should be reason to assume that the immigrant will continue his criminal activities in the country or the crime should be so serious that he could not be allowed to remain. For the court to conclude that an immigrant has the propensity to commit additional crimes, a prior criminal record is usually a prerequisite. Serious crimes of violence, sex crimes and drug offenses are grounds for expulsion without a prior record. In fact, under Swedish practice, an offense that warrants imprisonment for at least one year will normally justify the expulsion of the offender.

The Swedish courts weigh the conflicting interests of the state and the individual in a manner similar to the balancing test performed by the ECHR under Article 8 of the European

---

[141] *Üner v. the Netherlands*, 45 EHRR 14, §5 (2007), *available at* http://www.bailii.org/eu/cases/ECHR/2006/873.html (holding "While a number of Contracting States have enacted legislation or adopted policy rules to the effect that long-term immigrants who were born in those States or who arrived there during early childhood cannot be expelled on the basis of their criminal record (see paragraph 39 above), such an absolute right not to be expelled cannot, however, be derived from Article 8 of the Convention, couched, as paragraph 2 of that provision is, in terms which clearly allow for exceptions to be made to the general rights guaranteed in the first paragraph.").

[142] Swedish Aliens Act of 2005, SFS 2005:716 (Sept. 29, 2005) and Act amending the Aliens Act, 2009, SFS 2009:1542 (Dec. 30, 2009). For an English summary of the 2005 Act and its 2009 Amendments, visit the Government of Sweden website: http://www.sweden.gov.se/sb/d/5805/a/66122.

[143] Swedish Penal Code, Chapter 29, § 5(4).

[144] Swedish Aliens Act, Ch. 8, § 8.

Convention. The Aliens Act stipulates that the court shall consider the immigrant's general life situation, including whether she has children in Sweden who need her, her other family ties and her length of stay in Sweden.[145] Other factors include the immigrant's housing and work situation and other signs of integration into Swedish society, such as knowledge of the Swedish language. Family ties carry great weight, especially if a spouse or a child is a Swedish citizen.

The immigrant's length of stay is a particularly important factor under Swedish law. If she has been in Sweden legally for five or more years – or four years since being granted permanent residency – she can only be expelled for exceptional reasons.[146] But a child who has come to Sweden before turning 15 and who has lived in Sweden for at least five years cannot be expelled at all.[147]

Law School Clinics in South Africa

Law school clinics can help fill a need for defender services, while also providing law students with practical legal skills. Student engagement in criminal defense clinics may also encourage law students to pursue careers in criminal defense or at least have an appreciation for the importance of effective criminal defense in the legal system.

In **South Africa**, there are several law school clinics operating with a variety of important partners. The University of Witwatersrand's Wits Law Clinic was created approximately twenty years ago and is one of the biggest law school clinics in South Africa. In 1994, the Wits Law Clinic entered into a partnership agreement with the South African Legal Aid Board.[148]

The University of Johannesburg's law school also has a clinical program. It operates a variety of clinics, including the Johannesburg Courts Clinic, which exists through a partnership with the South African Department of Justice. In exchange for alleviating caseloads and improving legal services to the general public, the clinic has access to the Department of Justice's facilities.[149] The clinic has four locations in the Central Divorce Court, the Inquests Court, the Centre for Juvenile Offenders in the Johannesburg Magistrate's Court and the Office for Family Violence.[150] Students at these clinics provide advice to clients and also draft case pleadings, notices and other documents.[151]

The law school clinic at University of KwaZulu-Natal also has an established legal clinic. The clinic operates a version of the popular American Street Law program developed by Professor

---

[145]*Id*. Ch. 8, §11(1).

[146] *Id*. Ch. 8, § 12. Exceptional circumstances include an offence that entails serious danger to public order and security, including a danger to national security. *See id*. at § 11.

[147] *Id*.

[148] University of Witwatersrand, Johannesburg, Wits Law Clinic, *available at* http://www.wits.ac.za/lawclinic/11045/witslawclinic.html.

[149] University of Johannesburg Law Clinic, http://www.uj.ac.za/EN/Faculties/law/about/Pages/LawClinic.aspx.

[150] *Id*.

[151] *Id*.

David McQuoid-Mason.[152] In the program law school students volunteer their time, sometimes for school credit, to teach school children, prisoners and communities about their legal rights.[153] Another component of the clinic is to provide legal aid, which is primarily civil and juvenile-related.[154] This opportunity provides law students with practical experience and also provides indigent clients with an additional resource in the community.

Restorative Justice for Aboriginal Communities in Canada

For traditional and Aboriginal communities, western notions of criminal justice may not be the best fit. Instead, communities might be strengthened by adopting alternative methods of seeking to restore justice by more directly focusing on the victim and the harm done to the community while protecting the rights of the accused. While no formal definition of restorative justice exists, NIJ held a series of symposia in the late 1990s that offered a variety of working definitions.[155]

Based on these symposia, NIJ has characterized the concept as follows:

> Restorative justice principles offer more inclusive processes and reorient the goals of justice. Restorative justice has been finding a receptive audience, as it creates common ground which accommodates the goals of many constituencies and provides a collective focus. The guiding principles of restorative justice are:
>
> - Crime is an offense against human relationships;
> - Victims and the community are central to justice processes;
> - The first priority of justice processes is to assist victims;
> - The second priority is to restore the community, to the degree possible;
> - The offender has personal responsibility to victims and to the community for crimes committed;
> - Stakeholders share responsibilities for restorative justice through partnerships for action;
> - The offender will develop improved competency and understanding as a result of the restorative justice experience.[156]

Canada has invoked restorative justice processes with its Aboriginal communities. Two of these processes that have received considerable attention are Sentencing Circles and Gladue Courts.

The more common of the two is alternative sentencing known as **Sentencing Circles**, which allows communities to intervene in criminal justice matters.[157] In order to access this alternative

---

[152] For more information on the Street Law model, visit http://www.streetlaw.org/en/index.aspx.

[153] University of KwaZulu-Natal, Street Law Program webpage, *available at* http://law.ukzn.ac.za/StreetLawProgramme.aspx.

[154] University of KwaZulu-Natal, Law Clinic webpage, *available at* http://law.ukzn.ac.za/LawClinic.aspx.

[155] *See* National Institute of Justice, Working Definition of Restorative Justice webpage, *available at* http://www.ojp.usdoj.gov/nij/topics/courts/restorative-justice/definitions1.htm.

[156] *See* National Institute of Justice, Restorative Justice webpage, *available at* http://www.ojp.usdoj.gov/nij/topics/courts/restorative-justice/welcome.htm.

sentencing process, the accused must plead guilty to an offense. Sentencing Circles may also require offenders to confess to other crimes that were not the focus of the particular investigation, which can create due process violations. For example, if a Sentencing Circle can be accessed by an individual accused of child sex abuse, not only must the individual plead guilty to the offense that has brought him or her to the attention of the authorities, but the defendant must also plead guilty to all other unreported and detected incidents against a child.[158]

Sentencing Circles are essentially conversations between the victim, offender and their families with members of the community present as facilitators. They proceed without the presence of a judge, prosecutor, defense attorney or other court personnel in the room. The primary objectives are to initiate a healing process between the victim and offender so they can move on from the offense and continue to live in the same community and to produce a more relevant and culturally informed sentence for the offender.

Researchers find that in these types of processes, the primary motive for defense lawyers to encourage their clients to enter into a Sentencing Circle process is to avoid incarceration. This often creates a conflict for the lawyer as they ask their clients to give up important due process rights for the opportunity to receive a potentially non-incarcerative sentence. However, often after the offender enters into the Sentencing Circle process, the risk-need profile presented by the offender through his or her own testimony is not conducive to a non-incarcerative sentence. Thus, the offender will have to be sentenced to a program outside of the community given that only a few Aboriginal communities have services to support community-based sentencing, such as drug and alcohol treatment or other health or social services.

Measuring the effectiveness of these Sentencing Circles is somewhat difficult. One Sentencing Circle in Canada claimed that it reduced recidivism by 80%.[159] However, the Canadian government has not formally evaluated these processes so far. The Australian Institute of Criminology (AIC) has conducted an evaluation of Sentencing Circles in **Australia** and found that they have not made an impact on recidivism.[160] Instead, AIC found that the best predictor of an offender's future behavior is past behavior.

Other researchers have found that Sentencing Circles probably benefit offenders more than victims. An unfortunate, but frequent result is re-victimization of the injured. Moreover, while

---

[157] For more information on Sentencing Circles in Canada, *see* Jane Dickson-Gilmore & Carol LaPrairie, *Will the Circle Be Unbroken?: Aboriginal Communities, Restorative Justice, and the Challenges of Conflict and Change* (2005).

[158] This is the experience reported out of the "Community Holistic Circle Healing" program being administered in the community of Hollow Water, Manitoba. *See* Therese Lajeunesse, *Evaluation of the Hollow Water Community Holistic Circle Healing Project,* Ottawa: Solicitor General Canada, 1996; Native Counselling Services of Alberta, *A Cost-Benefit Analysis of Hollow Water's Community Holistic Circle Healing Process* (Ottawa: Solicitor General, Aboriginal Peoples' Collection no. 20, 2001).

[159] Robin J. Wilson, Franca Cortoni, & Andrew J. McWhinnie, "Circles of Support & Accountability: A Canadian National Replication of Outcome Findings," 21(4) *Sex Abuse* (2009), 412-430.

[160] Jacqueline Fitzgerald, "Does Circle Sentencing Reduce Aboriginal Offending?" 115 *Crime and Justice Bulletin* (May 2008), 1-2.

the community members often report feeling empowered at the start of the process, the end result is often one in which promises are not fully kept and follow-up is difficult to conduct.[161]

Another restorative justice model used in Canada for Aboriginal communities is problem-solving courts staffed with Aboriginal community members. The most common problem-solving court in Canada is the **Gladue Court**.[162] In Gladue Courts, court-personnel obtain extensive training on Aboriginal communities and the possible reasons why individuals from these communities are overrepresented in the criminal justice system. The Gladue workers create a comprehensive pre-sentencing report, which includes information obtained through meetings conducted with family and community members. They then work with offenders to help resolve problems and to prevent recidivism. The pre-sentencing report includes a risk-needs assessment to consider the resources the individuals need to overcome their problems. To date, evaluations of Gladue Courts indicate that they work well and are cost effective.[163]

---

[161] *See* Jane Dickson-Gilmore & Carol LaPrairie, *Will the Circle Be Unbroken?: Aboriginal Communities, Restorative Justice, and the Challenges of Conflict and Change* (2005) at 133-153.

[162] For more information on Gladue Courts, visit this page administered by the Community Legal Education Ontario http://www.cleonet.ca/resources/1042; *also* visit the Aboriginal Legal Services of Toronto website at http://www.web.net/~alst/.

[163] For example, in Toronto, the Gladue Court costs only $500,000 over three years. *See* Aboriginal Legal Services of Toronto (ALST) Evaluation of Gladue Courts (Years 1, 2, 3), *available at* http://www.aboriginallegal.ca/gladue.php.

APPENDIX B: AGENDA

Monday, January 24, 2011

8:30 – 9:00   **Registration, Networking Coffee and Continental Breakfast**

9:00 – 9:15   **Opening Remarks**
National Institute of Justice Director Dr. John H. Laub
Associate Attorney General Thomas Perrelli

9:15 – 9:25   **Workshop Goals and Outcomes**
Ed Connors, President, Institute for Law and Justice, Workshop Facilitator

The facilitator will provide instruction on the roundtable format and the direction, goals, and outcomes of the workshop.

9:25 – 11:00   **Framing the Issue: Indigent Defense in the United States**

Presentations
- ❖ Prof. Randolph Stone, University of Chicago School of Law
- ❖ Jo-Ann Wallace, President & CEO, NLADA
- ❖ Christina Swarns, Director of Criminal Justice Practice, NAACP – LDF
- ❖ Virginia Sloan, President & Founder, The Constitution Project

Facilitated Roundtable Discussion
Participants will have an opportunity to discuss their goals for the workshop and the questions they would like to explore over the course of the day and a half.

11:00 – 11:15   Break

11:15 – 12:45   Costs Associated with Being Indigent in the Criminal Justice System

Presentations
- ❖ Tapio Lappi-Seppala, Director, National Research Institute of Legal Policy - Finland
- ❖ Brian Ostrom, Principal Court Research Consultant, National Center for State Courts
- ❖ Nicholas Green, QC, Immediate Past Chairman, English Bar Council
- ❖ Prof. David Bruck, Washington & Lee School of Law

Facilitated Roundtable Discussion
This panel will explore the economic and non-economic costs associated with incarcerating and sentencing low-income individuals convicted of crimes across a variety of jurisdictions. Discussion will focus on how poverty amplifies such issues as the rate of incarceration in different jurisdictions and the costs associated with incarceration and sentences such as the death penalty.

12:45 – 2:00   Lunch
Lynn Overmann, Deputy Counselor for Access to Justice
Assistant Attorney General Laurie Robinson
Keynote Speaker: Chief Justice Margaret Marshall (ret.)

2:00 – 3:30   Improvements to the Provision of Defender Services for the Poor

Presentations
- ❖ Prof. Norm Lefstein, Indiana University School of Law-Indianapolis
- ❖ Zaza Namoradze, Director of Budapest Office, Open Society Justice Initiative
- ❖ Thomas Giovanni, Director, Community Oriented Defender Network, Brennan Center for Justice
- ❖ Michael Karnavas, International Criminal Defense Lawyer

Facilitated Roundtable Discussion
Panelists will discuss innovations that have improved the provision of defender services to low-income individuals both domestically and abroad.

3:30 – 3:45   Break

3:45 – 5:00   The Intersection of Indigent Defense and Immigration

Presentations
- ❖ Prof. John Rubin, UNC-Chapel Hill School of Government
- ❖ Anders Mansson, Head of Division, European Court of Human Rights

Facilitated Roundtable Discussion
This panel will discuss the effects of the intersection of immigration and criminal law on indigent defense, both domestically and abroad.

5:00 – 5:30   Highlights from the Day

In this facilitated roundtable, participants will have a chance to comment on the day's highlights and discuss the research questions raised in presentations and discussions.

5:30   Adjourn Day 1

Tuesday, January 25, 2011

8:00 – 8:25   Networking Coffee and Continental Breakfast

8:25 – 8:30   Welcome
Deborah Leff, Deputy Counselor for Access to Justice

8:30 – 10:00   Improvements for Juveniles

Presentations
- ❖ Robert Schwartz, Executive Director, Juvenile Law Center
- ❖ Prof. Ton Liefaard, University of Utrecht
- ❖ Prof. Thomas Geraghty, Bluhm Legal Clinic, Northwestern University School of Law
- ❖ Patricia Puritz, Executive Director, National Juvenile Defender Center

Facilitated Roundtable Discussion
This panel will discuss the special problems children of low-income families encounter when they are involved in the criminal justice system and alternative international practices to address juvenile justice.

10:00 – 10:10   Break

10:10 – 11:30   Indigent Defense in Indigenous Communities

Presentations
- ❖ John Harte, Partner, Mapetsi Policy Group
- ❖ Prof. Ron Whitener, Director, Tribal Court Criminal Defense Clinic, University of Washington School of Law
- ❖ Prof. Jane Dickson-Gilmore, Carleton University- Ottawa

Facilitated Roundtable Discussion
Panelists will discuss the unique situations faced by indigenous communities in providing access to justice for the accused in tribal and national criminal justice systems. The panel will also cover informal or traditional justice mechanisms.

11:30 – 11:40   Facilitator Review of Panels and Discussion Highlights

11:40 – 11:55   Break

11:55 – 1:15   What Research is Needed?

Breakout Sessions
Participants will be divided into moderated roundtable discussions to discuss highlights and research needs.

Facilitated Review of Breakout Sessions
The groups will come together to discuss major points of interest to explore in research and to propose a new research agenda.

1:15   Adjourn Day 2

APPENDIX C: LIST OF PARTICIPANTS

Duren Banks
Chief, Prosecution and Adjudication
Statistics Unit
Bureau of Justice Statistics
U.S. Department of Justice
Washington, DC

Marlene Beckman
Counselor, Office of the Assistant
Attorney General
Office of Justice Programs
U.S. Department of Justice
Washington, DC

Ira Belkin
Program Officer, Law and Rights
The Ford Foundation, Beijing
Office
Beijing, China

David Bruck
Professor
Washington and Lee University
School of Law
Lexington, VA

Melanca Clark
Senior Counsel
Access to Justice Initiative
U.S. Department of Justice
Washington, DC

Cait Clarke
Director, Federal Programs
Equal Justice Works
Washington, DC

Edward Connors
President
Institute for Law and Justice
Alexandria, VA

Robin Dahlberg
Senior Staff Attorney, Racial Justice
Program/National Legal Staff
American Civil Liberties Union
New York, NY

Jane Dickson-Gilmore
Associate Professor
Carleton University
Ottawa, Canada

Joshua Dohan
Director
Youth Advocacy Department
Roxbury, MA

Donald Farole
Statistician, Prosecution and
Adjudication Statistics Unit
Bureau of Justice Statistics
U.S. Department of Justice
Washington, DC

Nadine Frederique
Social Science Analyst
National Institute of Justice
U.S. Department of Justice
Washington, DC

Thomas Geraghty
Associate Dean for Clinical
Education, Professor of Law
Director, Bluhm Legal Clinic
Northwestern University
School of Law
Chicago, IL

Thomas Giovanni
Director of the Community Oriented
Defender Network
Brennan Center for Justice
New York, NY

Jon Gould
Director, Washington Public Policy
Research Institute
American University
Washington, DC

Martin Gramatikov
Assistant Professor
Tilburg University
Tilburg, The Netherlands

Kathi Grasso
Senior Juvenile Justice Policy and
Legal Advisor, Office of Juvenile
Justice and Delinquency Prevention
U.S. Department of Justice
Washington, DC

Nicholas Green
Immediate Past Chairman of the Bar
English Bar Council
London, United Kingdom

Mary Greer
Senior Criminal Law Advisor
ABA Rule of Law Initiative
Washington, DC

John Harte
Partner
Mapetsi Policy Group
Washington, DC

Sam Hirsch
Deputy Associate Attorney General
Office of the Assistant Attorney
General
U.S. Department of Justice
Washington, DC

Benita Jain
Co-Director
Immigrant Defense Project
New York, NY

Miranda Jolicoeur
International Liaison and Research
Analyst (MetaMetrics, Inc.
Contractor)
International Center
National Institute of Justice
U.S. Department of Justice
Washington, DC

Joseph Jones
Senior Counsel for Rule of Law
Office of the Deputy Attorney
General
U.S. Department of Justice
Washington, DC

Maha Jweied
Senior Counsel
Access to Justice Initiative
U.S. Department of Justice
Washington, DC

Michael Karnavas
International Criminal Defense
Lawyer
The Hague, The Netherlands

Tapio Lappi-Seppala
Director
National Research Institute of Legal
Policy - Finland
Helsinki, Finland

Steven Lang
Coordinator, Legal Orientation and
Pro Bono Program
Executive Office for Immigration
Review
Falls Church, VA

Karen Lash
Senior Counsel
Access to Justice Initiative
U.S. Department of Justice
Washington, DC

Deborah Leff
Deputy Counselor for Access to
Justice
Access to Justice Initiative
U.S. Department of Justice
Washington, DC

Norman Lefstein
Professor of Law and Dean
Emeritus
Indiana University School of Law -
Indianapolis
Indianapolis, IN

Kirsten Levingston
Program Officer, Reforming Civil
and Criminal Justice Systems
The Ford Foundation
New York, NY

Ton Liefaard
Assistant Professor
University of Utrecht
Willem Pompe Institute for
Criminal Law and Criminology
Utrecht, The Netherlands

Katayoon Majd
Program Officer for Criminal and
Juvenile Justice
Public Welfare Foundation
Washington, DC

Anders Mansson
Head of Division,
Human Rights Chamber
European Court of Human Rights
Strasbourg, France

**Chief Justice Margaret Marshall
(ret.)**
Supreme Judicial Court of
Massachusetts
Boston, MA

Vivek Maru
Senior Counsel, Justice Reform
Practice Group
The World Bank
Washington, DC

Mary Meg McCarthy
Executive Director
Heartland Alliance's National
Immigrant Justice Center
Chicago, IL

Maureen McGough
Outreach Coordinator
National Institute of Justice
U.S. Department of Justice
Washington, DC

Liz McGrail
Legal Director
Capital Area Immigrants Rights
Coalition
Washington, DC

Joanne Moore
Director
Washington State Office of Public
Defense
Olympia, WA

Zaza Namoradze
Director, Budapest Office
Open Society Justice Institute
Budapest, Hungary

Daniel Olmos
Senior Counsel
Access to Justice Initiative
U.S. Department of Justice
Washington, DC

Brian Ostrom
Principal Court Research Consultant
National Center for State Courts
Williamsburg, VA

Lynn Overmann
Deputy Counselor for Access to
Justice, Access to Justice Initiative
U.S. Department of Justice
Washington, DC

Patricia Puritz
Executive Director
National Juvenile Defender Center
Washington, DC

JoAnne Richardson
Senior Program Manager
National Center for State Courts
Arlington, VA

Jane L. Ross
Director, Committee on Law and
Justice
The National Research Council
Washington, DC

John Rubin
Professor of Public Law and
Government, School of Government
University of North Carolina-
Chapel Hill
Chapel Hill, NC

Robert Schwartz
Executive Director
Juvenile Law Center
Philadelphia, PA

Virginia Sloan
President & Founder
The Constitution Project
Washington, DC

Robin Steinberg
Executive Director
The Bronx Defenders
Bronx, NY

Randolph Stone
Clinical Professor of Law
University of Chicago
School of Law
Chicago, IL

Christina Swarns
Director of the Criminal Justice
Practice
NAACP Legal Defense Fund
New York, NY

Danica Szarvas-Kidd
Policy Advisor for Adjudication
Bureau of Justice Assistance
U.S. Department of Justice
Washington, DC

Jo-Ann Wallace
President & Chief Operating Officer
National Legal Aid & Defender
Association
Washington, DC

Ron Whitener
Director, Tribal Court Public
Defense Clinic
University of Washington School of
Law
Seattle, WA

Wendy Young
Executive Director
Kids in Need of Defense
Washington, DC

Lin Zhu
China University of Political
Science and Law
International Visiting Scholar
American University
Washington College of Law
Washington, DC

APPENDIX D: RECENT DOJ EFFORTS AND FUNDED RESEARCH ON INDIGENT DEFENSE

ACCESS TO JUSTICE INITIATIVE (ATJ) http://www.justice.gov/atj/

❖ *Indigent Defense*
A key priority of the Access to Justice Initiative is working with national indigent-defense advocacy groups and public defenders from across the country to address the crisis in the provision of indigent legal defense. The Initiative's strategic goals in this area include expanding research on the delivery of indigent defense, encouraging comprehensive planning and reform, increasing training and technical assistance for defender programs, strengthening juvenile justice and supporting tribal courts. For more information on the Access to Justice Initiative, visit http://www.justice.gov/atj/.

OFFICE OF JUSTICE PROGRAMS (OJP) http://www.ojp.usdoj.gov/

❖ *DOJ National Symposium on Indigent Defense held February 18-19, 2010*
Symposium Materials available at: http://www.ojp.usdoj.gov/BJA/topics/inddef_index.html

---

NATIONAL INSTITUTE OF JUSTICE (NIJ) http://www.ojp.usdoj.gov/nij/

❖ *NIJ 2010 Conference, Keynote Address by Laurence Tribe, former Senior Counselor for Access to Justice.* Discussing indigent defense in the United States. Video of Keynote Speech available at:
http://nij.ncjrs.gov/multimedia/video-nijconf2010-keynote-tribe.htm

❖ *International Perspectives on Wrongful Convictions Report (Sept. 2010)* This report provides an overview of the participants' discussions at the International Perspectives on Wrongful Convictions Workshop held in September 2010. Report available at: http://www.nij.gov/topics/courts/sentencing/international-perspective-on-wrongful-convictions.pdf

❖ *Implementation and Impact of Indigent Defense Standards. (Dec. 2003)*
(NIJ grant recipient: National Legal Aid and Defender Association)
This report discusses the impact of indigent defense standards in assessing the need for standardization of this constitutionally mandated governmental service. Report available at:
http://www.ncjrs.gov/pdffiles1/nij/grants/205023.pdf

BUREAU OF JUSTICE ASSISTANCE (BJA) http://www.ojp.usdoj.gov/BJA/

❖ *BJA Projects and Programs on Indigent Defense*
http://www.ojp.usdoj.gov/BJA/topics/IndigentDefense.pdf

❖ *Public Defense Reform Since Gideon: Improving the Administration of Justice By Building On Our Successes and Learning From Our Failures: A Public Defense Leadership Focus Group (2008)*
(BJA grant recipient: American University Criminal Courts Technical Assistance Project and American University Criminal Courts Technical Assistance Project). This report provides a summary of focus group discussions held to review the successes and failures in the delivery of public defense services and assess the lessons learned resulting in recommendations for the future. Report available at:
http://www.ojp.usdoj.gov/BJA/pdf/NLADA_PubDefLeadership.pdf

❖ *What Policymakers Need To Know To Improve Public Defense Systems (Dec. 2001)*
(BJA grant recipient: Harvard University, John F. Kennedy School of Government). One in a series of papers developed by the Executive Session on Public Defense, a 30-member effort with leading figures in public defense. In This paper sets out questions to aid policymakers in assessing the value and effectiveness of their public defense systems. Paper available at:
http://www.ncjrs.gov/pdffiles1/bja/190725.pdf

❖ *Keeping Defender Workloads Manageable (2001)*
(BJA grant recipient: The Spangenberg Group)
This report discusses approaches developed by public defender organizations, state legislatures, state courts and other entities to managing the workloads of attorneys who represent indigent defendants. Report available at: http://www.ncjrs.gov/pdffiles1/bja/185632.pdf

❖ *Contracting for Indigent Defense: Special Report (2000)*
(BJA grant recipient: The Spangenberg Group)
Written for individuals in the justice system who are using, considering or implementing an indigent defense contract system, this report presents the major judicial and legislative attempts to deal with those systems, examines the best and worst features of contract systems and discusses the national standards that govern contract systems. Report available at: http://www.ncjrs.gov/pdffiles1/bja/181160.pdf

❖ *Indigent Defense and Technology: A Progress Report (1999)*
(BJA grant recipient: The Spangenberg Group)
This report looks at how technology is changing the way attorneys and staff work in public defender offices. Report available at: http://www.ncjrs.gov/pdffiles1/bja/179003.pdf

BUREAU OF JUSTICE STATISTICS (BJS) http://bjs.ojp.usdoj.gov/

❖ *County-based and Local Public Defender Offices (2007)*
This BJS produced report examines the provision of public defender services in the 27 states and the District of Columbia in which indigent defense services were funded and administered by counties or local jurisdictions in 2007. Report available at: http://bjs.ojp.usdoj.gov/index.cfm?ty=pbdetail&iid=2211

❖ *State Public Defender Programs (2007)*
This BJS produced report examines the provision of public defender services in the 22 States that had an entirely State-funded and State-administered indigent defense program in 2007. Report available at: http://bjs.ojp.usdoj.gov/index.cfm?ty=pbdetail&iid=2242

OFFICE OF JUVENILE DELINQUENCY AND PREVENTION (OJJDP) http://www.ojjdp.gov/

❖ *OJJDP FY 10 Juvenile Indigent Defense National Clearinghouse*
The National Juvenile Defender Center was awarded OJJDP funding to operate this clearinghouse:
http://www.njdc.info

❖ *OJJDP News At A Glance Article (March/April 2010)*
Summary of juvenile defender topics addressed at the 2010 DOJ National Symposium on Indigent Defense. Available at: http://www.ncjrs.gov/html/ojjdp/news_at_glance/229711/topstory.html

NATIONAL INSTITUTE OF CORRECTIONS, FEDERAL BUREAU OF PRISONS (NIC) http://nicic.gov/

❖ *Evidence-Based Practices and Criminal Defense: Opportunities, Challenges, and Practical Considerations (Aug. 2008)*
One in a set of papers focused on the role of system stakeholders in reducing offender recidivism through the use of evidence-based practices in corrections.
Available at: http://nicic.gov/library/files/023356.pdf